HOME REPAIR AND IMPROVEMENT

LANDSCAPING

TIME®
LIFE
BOOKS

Other Publications
THE TIME-LIFE COMPLETE GARDENER
JOURNEY THROUGH THE MIND AND BODY
WEIGHT WATCHERS® SMART CHOICE RECIPE COLLECTION
TRUE CRIME
THE AMERICAN INDIANS
THE ART OF WOODWORKING
LOST CIVILIZATIONS
ECHOES OF GLORY
THE NEW FACE OF WAR
HOW THINGS WORK
WINGS OF WAR
CREATIVE EVERYDAY COOKING
COLLECTOR'S LIBRARY OF THE UNKNOWN
CLASSICS OF WORLD WAR II
TIME-LIFE LIBRARY OF CURIOUS AND UNUSUAL FACTS
AMERICAN COUNTRY
VOYAGE THROUGH THE UNIVERSE
THE THIRD REICH
MYSTERIES OF THE UNKNOWN
TIME FRAME
FIX IT YOURSELF
FITNESS, HEALTH & NUTRITION
SUCCESSFUL PARENTING
HEALTHY HOME COOKING
UNDERSTANDING COMPUTERS
LIBRARY OF NATIONS
THE ENCHANTED WORLD
THE KODAK LIBRARY OF CREATIVE PHOTOGRAPHY
GREAT MEALS IN MINUTES
THE CIVIL WAR
PLANET EARTH
COLLECTOR'S LIBRARY OF THE CIVIL WAR
THE EPIC OF FLIGHT
THE GOOD COOK
WORLD WAR II
THE OLD WEST

*For information on and a full description of
any of the Time-Life Books series listed above,
please call 1-800-621-7026 or write:*
Reader Information
Time-Life Customer Service
P.O. Box C-32068
Richmond, Virginia 23261-2068

HOME REPAIR AND IMPROVEMENT

LANDSCAPING

BY THE EDITORS OF TIME-LIFE BOOKS, ALEXANDRIA, VIRGINIA

The Consultants

Guy Morgan Williams is a landscape architect whose experience ranges from small urban gardens to large-scale master plans and estate design. He is president and co-owner of DCA Landscape Architects, Inc., in Washington, D.C.

Mark M. Steele is a professional home inspector in the Washington, D.C., area. He has developed and conducted training programs in home-ownership skills for first-time homeowners. He appears frequently on television and radio as an expert in home repair and consumer topics.

CONTENTS

Plans and Preliminaries

Whether you are considering planting a single shrub or remaking your entire yard, successful landscaping begins with a well-thought-out plan. Besides forecasting results, it can show where improvements need to be made. Then, armed with the proper tools, you can level uneven ground, grade or terrace slopes, correct faulty drainage, and enrich soil in preparation for making your landscaping plan a reality.

A collection of gardening equipment represents a big investment and should be treated accordingly. Proper storage and maintenance will prolong the life of your tools. Moreover, simple repairs can often restore broken or aging equipment to full usefulness.

Basic Care: Tools should be kept indoors in a place free of rust-producing moisture; before putting them away, clean them and wipe them dry. Protect cutting tools against corrosion with a light application of household oil. Sharpen blades when they become dull. Carefully clean chemical sprayers after each use.

Easy Repairs: Typical troubles with a garden hose are treatable through surgery. If the hose develops a leak, remove the damaged section and make a splice with a mending kit; if a coupling is corroded or loose, cut it off and clamp a new one in place *(opposite)*. A tool with a broken handle can also be salvaged in almost all cases; replacement handles are generally available.

On shovels, rakes, hoes, and other lightweight garden tools, the new handle slides into a metal sleeve and is fastened with screws. The heads of heavy tools such as axes, sledgehammers, and mattocks have a collar that accommodates a thicker handle, and the repair also involves some extra steps *(page 11)*.

⚠️ **CAUTION** *Before removing a lawnmower blade to sharpen it, be sure to disconnect the motor's ignition wire from the spark plug to prevent inadvertent starting.*

TOOLS

Electric drill	Knife
Flat file	Screwdriver
Grinding stone drill	Small sledge-
attachment	hammer
Hammer	Whetstone

SAFETY TIPS

Wear gloves when cleaning any part of a sprayer, and wear goggles when sharpening metal blades and when hammering tool heads onto new handles.

SHARPENING PRUNING SHEARS AND MOWER BLADES

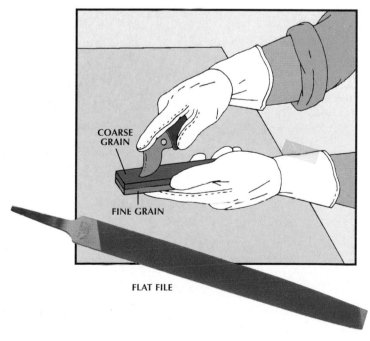

COARSE GRAIN

FINE GRAIN

FLAT FILE

Honing a pair of shears.
◆ Disassemble the shears by removing the hinge bolt.
◆ Put a few drops of light household oil or water on a whetstone's coarse side. Hold the beveled edge of the blade flush against the stone *(left)* and, starting at the tip, grind in small circles until the blade's edge is keen.
◆ Smooth the beveled edge by honing it on the whetstone's fine side with the same grinding motion. Reassemble the shears.
◆ You can also use a flat file *(photograph)* to sharpen shears: File the blade as described on the opposite page for a lawnmower blade.

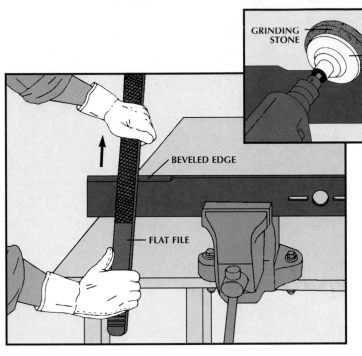

A keen edge for a lawnmower blade.

◆ Secure the blade in a vise. Lay a flat file flush with the beveled cutting edge *(left)*, and file in the direction indicated by the arrow; do not pull back. File evenly along the whole edge.

◆ When the edge looks shiny, file the burr off the underside. Sharpen the blade's other end the same way.

◆ Check for balance by hanging the blade on a nail sticking horizontally out of your workbench. If one end is heavier, sharpen it until the blade balances.

◆ To use a grinding stone drill attachment, place the nylon guide against the blade's underside *(inset)*.

◆ Turn on the drill and, holding the stone against the beveled edge, move it back and forth until the blade is sharp.

MENDING A HOSE

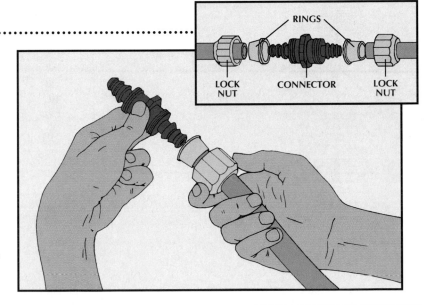

A splice to fix a leak.

◆ Cut out the leaking section of the hose. Soak the cut ends in hot water to soften the vinyl.

◆ Slip a lock nut from the mending kit over one cut end, with the nut's threads facing out toward the cut.

◆ Put a ring over the same end, then push the connector into the hose as far as it can go *(right)*. Slide the lock nut over the ring, and tighten the nut securely to the connector by hand.

◆ Repeat on the other end of the hose.

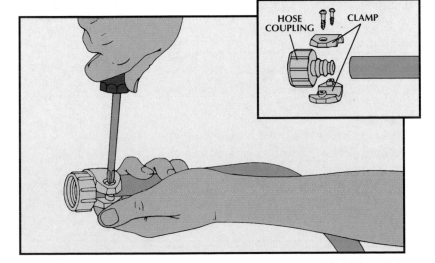

A new coupling for a hose end.

◆ Cut off the defective coupling. Push the new coupling into the cut end of the hose as far as it will go.

◆ Place the clamp halves around the hose at the base of the coupling, and screw the halves together to tighten the clamp *(right)*.

FLUSHING OUT A GARDEN-HOSE SPRAYER

Back-flushing the sprayer head.

◆ Remove the container from the sprayer head, leaving the head attached to the garden hose.

◆ Turn the control valve of the sprayer to ON, and cover the outlet hole with a finger *(right)*. Run water through the hose; the water will flush back through the sprayer and out of the suction tube, washing away chemical residues. Catch the water and residues in a separate container.

◆ Remove your finger from the outlet hole, and run water through the sprayer in the normal direction; if the hole is clogged, clear it with stiff wire.

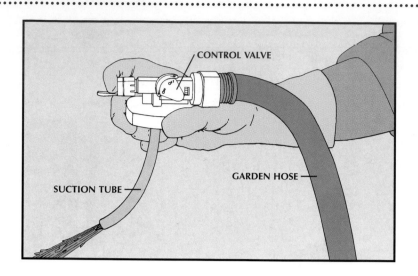

KEEPING A CANISTER SPRAYER CLEAN

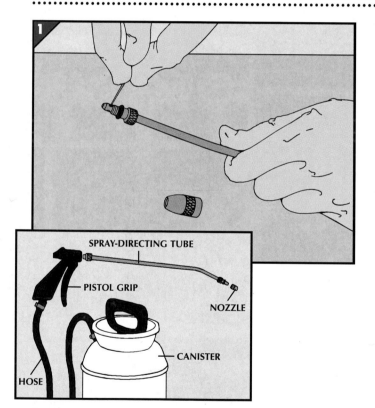

1. Clearing the outlet holes.

◆ Unscrew the spray-directing tube from the pistol grip, and remove the nozzle from the end of the tube.

◆ With a stiff wire, clear any residue from the outlet holes at the end of the tube *(above)*.

⚠ CAUTION

Handling Chemicals Safely

When cleaning sprayers, dump all rinse water into a separate container. Wrap paper around any wire and swabs used in the cleaning. Take the waste materials to your area's toxic waste pickup or disposal facility. Do not pour chemical wastes down the drain.

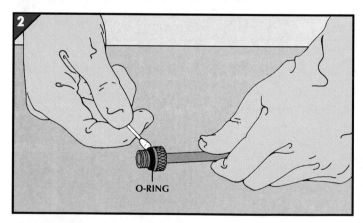

2. Completing the cleaning.

◆ Wipe the inside of the nozzle and the threads at the ends of the spray-directing tube with moistened cotton-tipped swabs until the cotton comes away clean.

◆ Lubricate the nozzle and threads with a swab dipped in household oil.

◆ With the swab, oil the O-rings at each end of the tube *(above)* to prevent sticking and maintain sealing power.

◆ Reassemble the sprayer and fill the canister with water. Spray the water to flush the hose and pistol grip.

A NEW HANDLE FOR A LARGE TOOL

COLLAR

1. Removing a damaged handle.
◆ Secure the head of a large tool, such as the mattock shown at left, in a heavy vise.
◆ With a $\frac{1}{4}$-inch bit, drill four deep holes into the wood at the top of the handle as close as possible to the collar.
◆ Remove the tool from the vise, and tap the head with a small sledgehammer, driving it down toward the narrow part of the handle. If the head remains stuck, drill additional holes and tap harder.

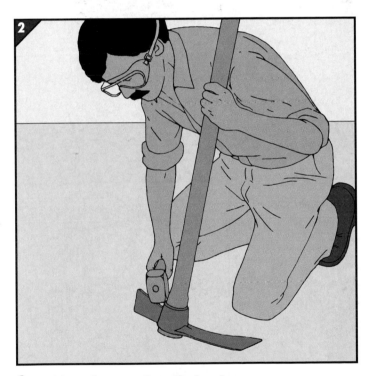

2. Setting the new handle in place.
◆ Slip the mattock head onto the new handle.
◆ Drive the head into position with a small sledgehammer, forcing it over the wide section at the top of the handle *(above)*; alternate the hammer blows from one side of the collar to the other to keep the head level.
◆ Set the mattock head in warm water overnight to swell the wood.

3. Making a tight fit.
◆ Let the wood dry. With a hammer, drive a $\frac{1}{2}$-inch metal wedge—available at hardware stores—into the top of the handle across the grain of the wood *(above)*. This should press the wood firmly against the collar.
◆ If the head of the tool is even slightly loose on the handle, drive additional wedges perpendicular to the first until the head is absolutely secure.

How to Be Your Own Landscape Designer

Like any major home-improvement project, landscaping calls for advance planning. Even a small lot is surprisingly flexible and warrants a systematic weighing of the design options that are available.

Making a Map: Begin by creating a map of your property—the more detailed the better *(page 16)*. Include such factors as pleasing views and existing plantings. Note the locations of underground obstacles such as electric, water, and sewer lines, or dry wells, septic tanks, and cesspools; they will prevent or limit digging in certain areas.

Planning the New Yard: Look at your lot as a whole and list all the important intended uses of your outdoor space—relaxation, storage, gardening, and so on. To some extent, the orientation of the house on the lot will define these areas: Traditionally, the house divides the lot into an approach area in the front yard; a private living area in the back; and an out-of-the-way service area, perhaps at the side of the house, for a set of trash cans or a toolshed. You may want to distinguish other areas—for games or work, say—and perhaps set them off with their own design elements.

Adding Design Touches: Once you have outlined these areas, experiment on paper with the look of each one, keeping in mind the design principles explained at right and on the following two pages. At this stage, think of plantings in terms of their general visual attributes *(below)* and such basic characteristics as whether they are evergreen or deciduous, flowering or nonflowering. Consider physical comfort in your planning. Hedges and fences can screen an area from the street or neighboring houses. A strategically placed tree will filter light or create shade and can lower the temperature on a patio by 15° to 20° F. A row of evergreen shrubs will shelter a walkway from winter winds. Choosing the specific plants that meet your criteria is the last step in the design process *(see appendix, pages 112 -125)*.

Visual Building Blocks

Each tree and shrub in a landscape has a number of visual attributes—shape, color, texture, scale (or size), proportions (the relationship between vertical and horizontal dimensions), and intensity of color. As you plan your design, picture how the visual qualities of the individual plantings will blend or contrast and how each tree or shrub might contribute to an overall feeling.

Design elements need to be considered not just individually but also in combinations. Terms such as *symmetry* or *balance* refer to their joint effects on the eye and mind.

SHAPE

COLOR

TEXTURE

SCALE

PROPORTION

INTENSITY

ASYMMETRY

SYMMETRY

BALANCE

A RANGE OF EFFECTS

Unity.

Arrange the elements of your yard to create a unified picture—one in which the viewer's eye travels easily over the various elements, seeing them as parts of a whole. At right, two different borders of trees and shrubs both have a harmonious effect: In the top arrangement, the various sizes and shapes blend together casually; at bottom, the pattern of small and large plantings has a more formal unity.

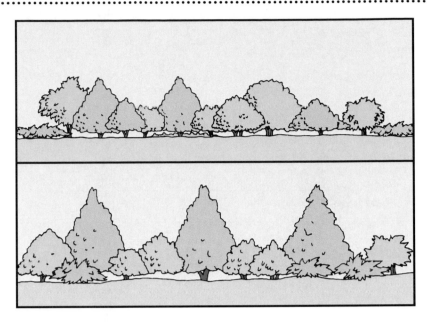

Focal point.

An element that attracts the eye is a focal point; it may be a door, bench, garden pool, arbor, specimen plant, or sculpture. Focal points are often at one end of a central axis, as at top left. The symmetrically planted flowers and shrubs accentuate the walk and draw the viewer's attention to the focal point—the front door.

Another way to highlight an element is to place it in an area where it stands out; this can be off-center, as with the bench at bottom left. The shape of the garden leads the eye to the bench—the focal point for this view.

Balance.

All landscape elements have a visual "weight." Good designs often balance their elements—large and small, light and dark, coarse and fine, dense and open—around a central point. In the asymmetrically balanced view at right, each side is different but the weights are similar: the group of shrubs balance the tall tree. A simpler route to balance would be through symmetry, designing a yard so that its two sides almost mirror each other.

Rhythm.

The repeated use of similar patterns or shapes creates a visual rhythm by drawing the eye from one area to the next. Here, the outlined elements—the rectangular paving blocks, the planting beds, and the two trees along one side of the yard—provide a pleasant sense of movement.

Contrast.

Alterations in materials, plants, textures, or lines can enliven a design. In this example, the stone path adds a new texture, and its curving shape breaks up the yard's straight lines. The vine-covered screen provides some variety because it contrasts with the rest of the fencing, and the different shapes of the trees also add interest.

Designing with geometry.

Geometrical arrangements of plantings and paving can play a major role in a landscape design. In the top example at left, rectangles and squares *(highlighted)* reflect and extend the straight architectural lines of the house. Curves *(middle)* do the opposite, posing a strong and intriguing contrast to the house lines. Triangles *(bottom)* direct the eye to a focal point—here, the expanse of lawn in the center.

DRAFTING A NEW PLAN

1. Mapping the site.

◆ On a sheet of graph paper, draw a map of your lot to scale. Then add a floor plan of the house's ground floor.

◆ Indicate good and bad views both from the windows of the house and from points within the yard; also note views into neighboring yards.

◆ Draw in existing trees, shrubs, flower beds, downspouts, and underground utilities; label steep banks, level areas, and spots with good drainage.

◆ Show the sun's morning, midday, and afternoon positions, as well as the direction of summer and winter winds.

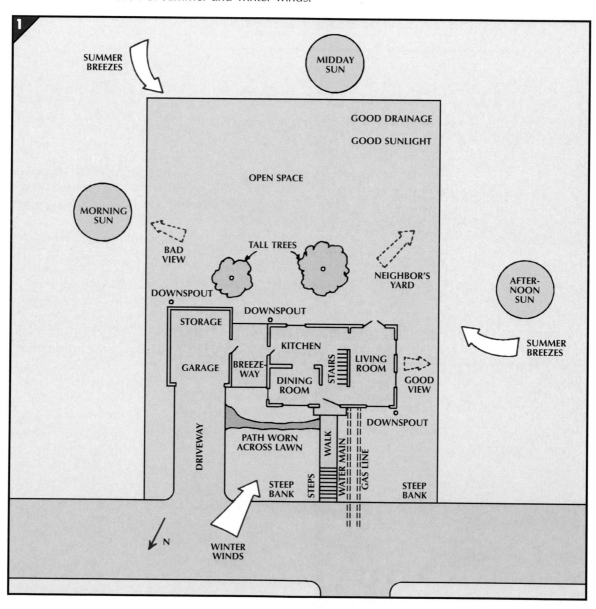

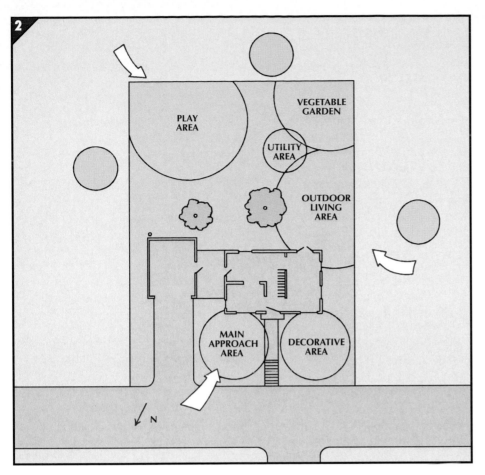

2. Outlining use areas.

◆ Tape tracing paper over the lot map and outline some use areas for the major sections of your yard.

◆ In the plan at left, the lawn near the driveway is designated as the main approach area; a path has already been worn there. The plan calls for decorative plantings that will screen the street view from inside the house. The space behind the living room is defined as an outdoor living area. A well-drained, sunny corner of the yard is envisioned as a vegetable garden, with an adjacent utility area for tool storage.

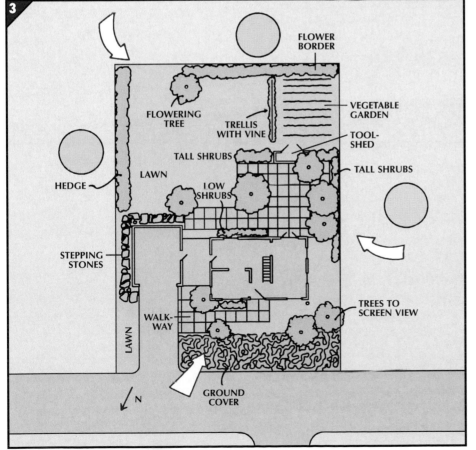

3. Experimenting with designs.

◆ Put a fresh sheet of tracing paper over your map, and experiment with designs for each of your circles on the previous map.

◆ Try to think of two or three different options for each area, remembering that you can remove things as well as add them. In the example at left, the old front steps are gone; instead, a paved walkway runs from the driveway to the front door. Decorative ground cover replaces hard-to-mow grass on the bank facing the street. In the backyard, the outdoor living area becomes a paved patio, and new shade trees and a high hedge block the afternoon sun and the neighbor's yard.

17

Many landscaping projects require that the contours of uneven ground be smoothed. Gardens, pools, patios, and playgrounds, for example, all need a level tract. Lawns, too, are more attractive and easier to maintain if they are relatively flat. Although some earth-moving jobs are extensive enough to warrant the hiring of an excavating company, a surprising amount of earth can be moved by hand, in short sessions of digging and hauling.

Clearing Away Obstacles: Stones, stumps, logs, and other large debris must be removed before a site can be leveled. If a rock is too massive to be moved by the technique that is shown on page 19, either call in professional excavators or modify your landscape design to incorporate it—as the centerpiece of a rock garden, for example *(pages 98-99)*.

Don't try digging out a large tree stump by hand. Rather, rent a stump grinder; burn the stump with a special chemical solution sold in garden-supply centers; or cut the stump off just below ground level, cover it with dirt, and let it decompose naturally.

Grading the Land: If a plot of land is perfectly flat, water will pool there during a rain. To ensure that water drains properly, grade the site so that it drops at least 1 inch vertically for every 4 horizontal feet. Make sure that the grade slopes away from the house.

If different parts of your yard slope in different directions, wait for a steady, heavy rain and observe the natural drainage patterns for an hour or so. Then establish the right grade for each part of the yard by the string-and-grid method described on pages 20-21.

Filling In Low Spots: If you purchase earth to top off a grade, buy topsoil—a mix of earth and fertilizers from which stones, wood chips, and other debris have been removed—rather than fill, which often contains dense chunks of clay as well as rocks. A cubic yard of soil will cover 300 square feet of ground to a depth of 1 inch.

Protecting Your Back: To avoid back injuries, lift heavy loads as much as possible with the muscles of your arms and legs. As a further precaution, wear a lower-back support—either a weightlifter's belt or a back-saver brace of the kind used by furniture movers.

TOOLS

Spade	Sod cutter
Garden rake	Line level
Metal rod or digging bar	Wooden stakes and string

MANAGING HEAVY LOADS WITHOUT STRAIN

The right way to wield a spade.

◆ Standing upright, set your foot atop the blade of the spade and force it deep into the earth.

◆ Place your hands in the positions that are shown in the second picture above, and push the top of the handle down, using the tool as a lever to dislodge the soil.

◆ Flex your knees and slide your lower hand down the handle for better leverage. Keeping your back as straight as possible, use your arms and legs to lift and pitch the soil *(third and fourth pictures)*.

A two-hand lift.

◆ Holding your torso erect, squat as close as possible to the load to be lifted *(left picture)*.
◆ Keep the load close to your body and stand up slowly, using your legs—not your back—for lifting force *(middle)*.
◆ To lessen strain on your back, hold the load close to your waist *(right)*. When you turn, move your entire body, without twisting your torso.

A one-hand lift.

◆ Bending your knees slightly and keeping your back straight, lean forward from the waist to reach the load.
◆ Using your legs for lifting power and keeping your shoulders level, raise your body upright to lift the load. Extend your free arm for balance.

Clearing logs from a site.

◆ With a sturdy, rigid rod or digging bar, maneuver the log onto a roller—a smooth, cylindrical piece of wood or a section of iron pipe.
◆ Tie a rope around the forward end of the log. Pull the log slowly over the roller, slipping additional rollers under the forward end to keep the log supported. As each roller comes free at the back, move it to the front.

Moving a rock.

◆ With a rod or digging bar, lever a heavy stone—up to 100 pounds—onto a sheet of heavy canvas or burlap.
◆ Grasp the cloth firmly at both corners of one end, and use your arm and leg muscles to drag the rock from the site.

LEVELING AND GRADING A PLOT OF LAND

1. Skimming sod from the surface.

With a sod cutter, remove the sod in strips from the area that will be leveled. If you intend to re-lay the sod on the plot after grading, gently roll up the strips, move them off the site, and unroll them again. Keep the sod well watered until you are ready for replanting.

2. Leveling ridges and depressions.

Working when the soil is neither wet nor dry but slightly moist, transfer the dirt from obvious high spots in the plot to low spots. After you drop each spadeful, use the blade's end to break up compacted soil into chunks 1 inch across or less.

3. Setting a slope with stakes and strings.

◆ Drive stakes at the four corners of the plot. The stakes at the lowest corners (generally farthest from the house) should be tall enough to roughly match the level of the highest corners' stakes.

◆ Tie a string to one of the higher-corner stakes and stretch it along the side of the plot to the lower-corner stake opposite. As a helper checks a line level *(photograph)* hung from the string, raise or lower the string as necessary to level it.

◆ Mark the lower stake at the level of the string.

LINE LEVEL

Move the string down the stake to set the desired slope *(page 18)*. Tie the string in place there.

◆ Repeat the procedure on the other side of the plot, then complete the boundary by tying lev-eled strings between the stakes at the top and the bottom of the plot.

4. Laying out a grid.

◆ Drive stakes at 6-foot intervals just outside the strings that mark the boundaries of the plot.

◆ Create a grid over the area by tying a string between each opposite pair of stakes, setting the string at the level of the boundary strings. Make sure that the grid strings are taut.

5. Grading the surface.

◆ Working in one 6-foot square at a time, use a heavy rake to break up the soil to the consistency of coarse sand and spread it parallel to the plane of the string grid.

◆ Smooth the plot with the flat top side of the rake. Remove the stakes and strings.

Professional landscapers define drainage as a two-stage process—the flow of water across the ground according to grade and the subsequent seepage of the water into the soil. In the first stage, rainwater can create problems in several ways: It can erode steep ground; it may flow to low areas and leave them soggy long after the rain has stopped; or it may pool around a house and perhaps find its way through the foundation.

A Low-Cost Fix for a Wet Basement: If a high water table or some other unseen problem is causing a wet basement, drainage professionals will have to be called in—but first check to see if the situation is simply a result of faulty surface drainage. In a 10-foot-wide zone around the house, the grade should drop at least 1 vertical inch for every horizontal foot.

Correct any insufficiency in the grade, and at the same time, use flexible plastic pipe to extend your gutter downspouts so that rainwater is channeled away from the house. Depending on the slope of your yard, the extension can end either in an underground dry well that traps and slowly disperses the water *(right)* or in a simple culvert that drains it away.

Managing Hill Runoff: To keep rainwater from collecting at the base of a gentle slope, divert the flow by constructing berms and swales—low earthen dams and shallow trenches *(opposite, bottom)*. For steeper slopes, the solution may be to terrace the land and build a retaining wall *(pages 24-27)*.

TOOLS
Line level
Sod cutter
Spade
Tamper
Tape measure

MATERIALS
Wooden stakes and string
Flexible nonperforated drainpipe
Downspout adapter
Splash block
Topsoil
Gravel

DIVERTING WATER FROM THE FOUNDATION

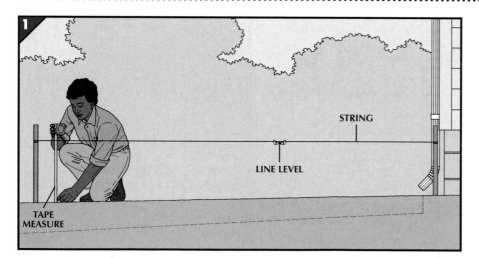

STRING

LINE LEVEL

TAPE MEASURE

1. Checking the grade.
◆ Drive a stake next to the house and another one 10 feet away from the foundation. Tie a string between them and level it with a line level. Measure from the string to the ground at 1-foot intervals to calculate the grade. Move the stakes and repeat at other points along one side of the house.

◆ In any area where the grade drops less than 1 vertical inch for each horizonal foot, strip the sod *(page 20)* and remove any shrubs *(page 64)*.
◆ Dig a trench for the downspout extension; the trench should be 8 inches wide, a minimum of 10 feet long, and at least 6 inches deep at the downspout. It should also slope 1 inch per foot *(dashed lines, above)*.

2. Extending the downspout.
◆ Attach an adapter to the end of the downspout.
◆ Lay flexible nonperforated drainpipe in the trench and connect it to the adapter. The pipe must lie flat along the bottom of the trench without any dips or humps. Remove or add dirt under the pipe as necessary.

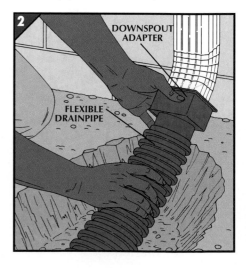

DOWNSPOUT ADAPTER

FLEXIBLE DRAINPIPE

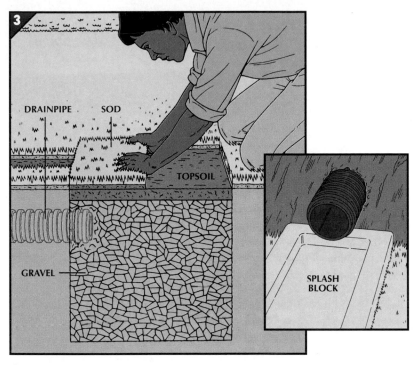

3. Making a dry well.

◆ At the end of the drainpipe trench, skim the sod from a $2\frac{1}{2}$-foot-square area and set it aside. Then dig a hole about 3 feet deep.

◆ Pull the flexible drainpipe so that the lip protrudes a few inches over the hole. Fill in the trench with topsoil and tamp it down.

◆ Fill the hole with gravel to a point about 1 inch above the top of the pipe. Add topsoil and replace the sod *(above)*.

◆ If the trench ends on a slope, lead the pipe out of the hill and onto a splash block *(inset)*. The block will prevent erosion at the outlet point.

4. Correcting the grade.

◆ When the drainpipe extension is complete, correct any improper grade around the house. If you are piling dirt higher against the foundation, first treat the masonry with a waterproofing sealant. The soil level must remain at least 6 inches below wooden siding in order to keep termites out.

◆ Use a tamper to pack the soil firmly.

CONTROLLING RUNOFF ON A GENTLE SLOPE

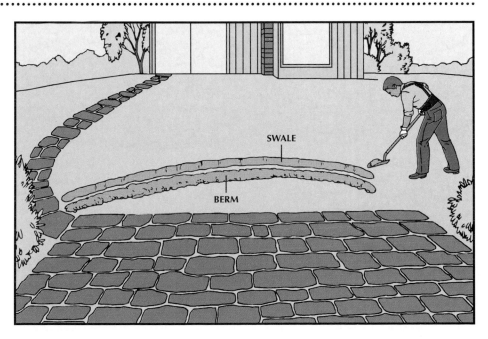

Creating berms and swales.

◆ Dig a trench, or swale, about 3 inches deep and at least twice that wide across the slope above the area you wish to protect. Create a berm by piling the leftover soil into a gently rounded mound below the swale, then tamp it down.

◆ Lay sod *(page 50)* on the berm and the swale or plant a ground cover *(page 51)*.

A Timber Retaining Wall

Terracing slopes with timber retaining walls not only solves erosion problems but can also add to the visual appeal of yards and gardens. Because earth and water create tremendous pressures behind a retaining wall, you must make the structure strong and provide for adequate drainage.

The design described at right and on the following pages meets these requirements; moreover, it is easy to build, presents a trim face unmarked by nails or fasteners, and in most localities requires no building permit. This design, however, is not suitable for walls that are more than 3 feet high; they call for both a permit and the services of a structural engineer. If you have a long, steep slope, consider terracing it at intervals with two or more 3-foot walls.

Choosing the Material: Wooden retaining walls can be made of any timbers that have been treated to resist rot and termites. Railroad ties were once the material of choice, but they have fallen out of favor because the wood is treated with the preservative creosote, which is poisonous to many plants.

Pressure-treated 6- by 6-inch timbers of poplar or pine, either rough- or smooth-sawed, are excellent alternatives. They are treated with environmentally safe preservatives and come in convenient 8-foot lengths, which can be cut as needed with a chain saw *(box, below)*.

Where to Place the Wall: If you build the wall near the bottom of the slope, as is the case here, you will need to add fill dirt behind it. Alternatively, you can excavate higher up, erect the wall against the slope's face, and cart away the leftover dirt. The first option increases your level yard space above the wall; the second, below it.

⚠ **CAUTION** *Before excavating, establish the locations of possible underground obstacles such as dry wells, septic tanks, and cesspools, and electric, water, and sewer lines.*

TOOLS

Line level
Shovel
Hand- or gas-
   powered tamper
Carpenter's level
Chain saw

Heavy-duty drill
   with a $\frac{3}{8}$-inch bit
   18 inches long
Long-handled
   sledgehammer

MATERIALS

Wooden stakes
   and string
Gravel
6-by-6 pressure-
   treated timbers of
   poplar or pine
Galvanized screen
   and nails

$\frac{3}{8}$-inch reinforcing
   steel bars 42
   inches long
$\frac{3}{8}$-inch galvanized
   spikes 12 inches
   long
4-inch perforated
   drain tile

Using a Chain Saw Safely

Be sure the cutting teeth are sharp and the chain is at the proper tension: You should never be able to pull it more than $\frac{1}{8}$ inch away from the bar. Steady the timbers on solid supports for sawing, and chalk cutting lines on the timbers as guides. Wear goggles to protect your eyes from flying woodchips. Brace the saw firmly on the ground before starting it, and hold the saw with both hands when cutting. Because pressure-treated lumber contains pesticides, wear a dust mask when sawing it and wash your hands thoroughly afterward.

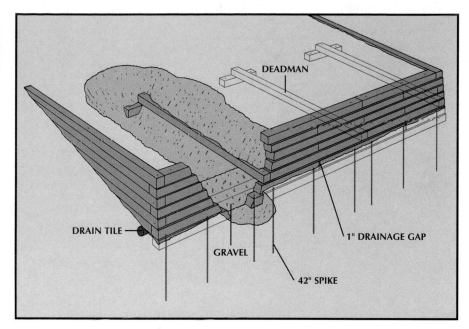

Anatomy of a retaining wall.

The bottom course in this 3-foot retaining wall is set in a trench and anchored by 42-inch-long bars of $\frac{3}{8}$-inch reinforcing steel, or rebar. Successive courses are secured with 12-inch galvanized spikes. Several features help the wall withstand the pressure of earth and water behind it. Each course is staggered $\frac{1}{2}$ inch toward the slope. Reinforcing timbers—deadmen–run 8 feet back into the hillside and rest on 1-foot-long timber crossplates anchored with 42-inch spikes. Sidewalls are built up on the corner deadmen and connected to the wall by interlocked corners. Four-inch perforated drain tile buried in gravel and 1-inch gaps between adjacent timbers in the second course provide escape routes for the water behind the wall.

PREPARING THE SITE

1. Marking the wall trench.

◆ Drive 5-foot stakes at the points you have chosen for the corners of the wall. Tie a line between the stakes, and level it with a line level.

◆ Measure to find the point where the line is farthest from ground level *(right)*. This is the lowest grade point; mark it with a stake.

◆ Drop a plumb line every 4 feet along the line, and drive stakes at these points to mark the outer edge of the wall. Transfer the line from the 5-foot stakes to the lower stakes.

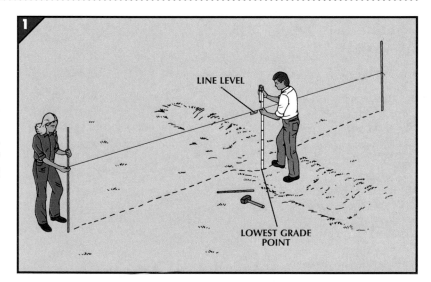

2. Digging the trench.

◆ Starting at the lowest grade point and working out to the corner stakes, dig a level-bottomed trench that is 1 foot deep at the lowest grade point and 1 foot wide along its full length.

◆ Spread a 6-inch layer of gravel in the trench and tamp it down. Check the base of the trench with a carpenter's level. Remove the stakes.

◆ Lay the timbers for the first course in the trench. Their tops should be even with ground level at the lowest grade point.

◆ To lay out deadman trenches, start at one corner and use the squaring method on page 84 to stretch an 8-foot line at right angles to the wall; drive a stake at the end of the line. Repeat at the other corner and at 6-foot intervals in between.

BUILDING THE WALL

1. Securing the first two courses.

◆ At the center of each timber and 6 inches from each end, drill vertical holes completely through, using the $\frac{3}{8}$-inch bit. Then drive 42-inch spikes through the holes and into the ground with a sledgehammer *(right)*.

◆ Lay the second course so that the joints between timbers do not coincide with those of the first. Set the second course $\frac{1}{2}$ inch closer to the hillside, and leave 1-inch gaps between timbers to serve as drainage holes.

◆ Drill three holes through each timber, and drive 12-inch spikes through the holes to pin the first two courses together.

2. Bracing the wall.

◆ For the deadmen, dig trenches—their bottoms level with the top of the second course—back to the stakes.

◆ Across the ends of the deadman trenches, dig crossplate trenches 3 feet long and 6 inches deeper than the deadman trenches at that point.

◆ Lay the crossplates in place, then set the deadmen on top of them so their other ends rest on the second course,

$\frac{1}{2}$ inch back from the front face. Drill pilot holes and drive 42-inch spikes through the deadmen and the crossplates and into the ground. Drive 12-inch spikes through the deadmen into the second course.

◆ For the third course of the wall, cut timbers to fit between the deadmen—making sure that the joints don't align with those of the second course—and secure them with spikes.

3. Laying a drainage run.

◆ On the back of the wall, nail pieces of galvanized screen over the drainage gaps in the second course of timbers.

◆ Shovel a bed of gravel behind the wall, leaving enough space to run a length of 4-inch perforated drain tile along the top of the bed and under the deadmen *(below)*. Then add another 6 inches of gravel.

4. Interlocking the corners.

◆ After completing the fourth course of timbers, lay a sidewall timber at each end of the wall and secure it to the corner deadman with 12-inch spikes.

◆ Lay another sidewall timber atop the first so that its end is set back $\frac{1}{2}$ inch from the face of the fourth course. Secure it with spikes.

◆ Fit the timbers for the fifth course between the sidewall timbers, fastening them with spikes.

◆ Continue laying the front and sidewall courses in this manner, making sure to offset the timber joints between courses and stagger each course $\frac{1}{2}$ inch closer to the hillside. Then drill horizontal holes through the corner deadmen and those sidewall courses that extend to the front of the wall, and drive 12-inch spikes to secure the corners *(right)*.

◆ Spread a 4-inch layer of soil behind the wall and tamp it with a hand- or gas-powered tamper. Spread and tamp additional 4-inch layers until the fill is level with the top of the wall.

Preparing Soil for Planting

All soils are composed primarily of mineral particles, ranging in size from fine, dense clay to medium-size silt to coarse, loose sand. The proportions of these ingredients—along with decayed vegetable and animal matter, known as humus—determine the texture and quality of the soil. Soil that has too much clay in it retains water almost indefinitely, causing problems with drainage. Sandy soil dries too quickly and allows nutrients to leach out.

The best garden soil is called loam and is a balance of clay, silt, and sand, with plenty of humus to help hold the mineral particles together and aid in the retention of moisture. Crumbly in texture, loam has plentiful spaces to let both air and excess water pass through, while nutrients are retained. Humus keeps the soil fertile and makes the soil easy to work.

Proper texture is only one requirement of good garden soil. In addition, the soil must contain nutrients necessary for plant growth, and it should be neither too acidic nor too alkaline—conditions that impair the ability of roots to extract the nutrients from the soil.

A Soil Diagnosis: With a few simple tests, you can evaluate your soil's texture and chemical composition. The water test shown at right can gauge the need for texture-improving organic amendments.

Peat moss and dehydrated manure are two widely used amendments, but the best of all is compost; it adds nutrients as well as improving soil structure—and you can make it in your backyard *(page 31)*.

For chemical tests, use an inexpensive soil-test kit, available at garden centers. Most of these kits contain an array of test vials and chemicals, along with charts for interpreting the results. There are tests for nitrogen, phosphorus, potassium, and—most important of all—the degree of acidity or alkalinity, known as pH.

Getting the Correct pH: The scale that measures pH runs from 0 to 14. Neutral soil has a pH of 7. Above 7, soil is increasingly alkaline; below 7, it is increasingly acid. Most plants grow best in slightly acid soil, with a pH level between 6 and 7; consult the appendix *(pages 112-125)* for plant preferences.

To reduce acidity, add dolomitic limestone, which includes magnesium, an essential nutrient. In light, sandy soil, 4 pounds per every 100 square feet will raise the pH by .5; add 20 percent to this formula for loamy soil and 30 percent in heavy, clayey soil.

Excess alkalinity is corrected by adding sulfur—either pure ground sulfur, iron sulfate, or aluminum sulfate. Pure sulfur acts more slowly than the others but lasts longer;

iron sulfate puts iron in the soil, producing lush, dark foliage; aluminum sulfate must be used cautiously because too much aluminum can be harmful to plants.

To reduce the alkalinity in 100 square feet of sandy soil by a pH interval of .5 to 1, use 3 to 5 pounds of iron or aluminum sulfate, or $\frac{1}{2}$ to $\frac{3}{4}$ pound of ground sulfur; use $1\frac{1}{2}$ times as much in loamy soil, 4 times as much in clayey soil.

When and How to Enrich the Soil: Add amendments to your soil 4 to 6 months before planting, to give them time to become thoroughly incorporated. Mix in organic amendments by tilling the soil *(page 30)*. Broadcast dolomitic limestone or sulfur on the surface, then rake it into the top few inches.

For a small area, you can do the tilling with a spade and spading fork *(page 30)*. To till a large area quickly and easily, rent a power tiller. A model that has the tines set behind the engine is more stable and generally preferable for a beginner; a model with tines mounted on the front is more maneuverable in tight places.

Do not till soggy soil; it will break up into large, heavy clods that can dry as hard as rocks. A good time for tilling is generally 3 days after a rain, when the soil is neither too wet nor so dry that the job creates annoying dust.

 **TOOLS**

Spade	Test kit
Bucket	Tarp
Trowel	Spading fork
Ruler	Power tiller

 **MATERIALS**

Manure
Peat moss
Compost
Dolomitic limestone
Sulfur

ANALYZING TEXTURE AND CHEMISTRY

1. Gathering samples.
◆ At several different spots within the area you intend to plant, dig holes about 6 inches wide and 6 to 9 inches deep.
◆ Slice a thin wedge of soil from the wall of each hole *(above)*. Wearing gloves so that your hands do not affect soil chemistry, remove sod and any small stones or roots from the samples, then mix them all together in a plastic bucket with the spade or a trowel.

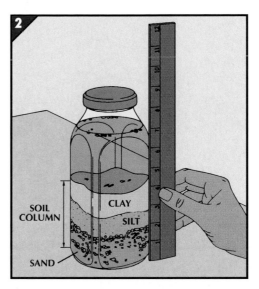

2. A water test for texture.
◆ Fill a quart bottle half full with water and add soil until the bottle is nearly full. Cap the bottle, shake it well, then wait for the soil particles to settle in layers—from 3 hours to a day.
◆ Measure the thickness of each layer—clay on top, silt in the middle, and sand on the bottom—and divide it by the total height of the soil column to get each component's percentage.
◆ When you adjust your soil's texture with organic amendments *(page 30)*, add about 2 or 3 inches of peat moss, manure, or compost if the soil is less than 25 percent silt or more than 25 percent clay. For soil that is more than 30 percent sand, add twice as much.

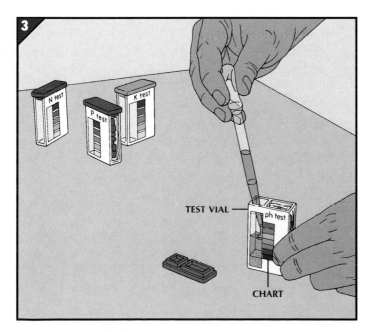

3. Testing the pH level.
◆ Fill the pH test chamber of a soil test kit to the correct mark with soil and add the amount of chemical called for in the kit's directions.
◆ Using an eyedropper, fill the chamber with water up to the indicated line *(left)*. Cap the chamber and shake it to mix the soil and the liquid thoroughly.
◆ After the soil particles settle, compare the color of the remaining solution with the kit's color chart. The closest match of colors indicates your soil's pH level.

SOIL AMENDMENTS

Turning the soil by hand.
◆ With the point of a spade, outline the area to be worked and divide it into sections 2 feet wide.
◆ Dig out the soil from an end section to the full depth of the spade (6 to 9 inches), depositing the soil on a plastic sheet or tarp *(above, left)*. Then fill this trench with soil from the adjacent section *(above, right)*.

◆ Spread the desired organic soil amendments *(Step 2, page 29)* on the first section and work them in with a spading fork.
◆ Transfer the top 9 inches of soil from the third section to fill up the second, and add amendments. Continue in this way until you reach the last section. Fill the last trench with the original soil from the first section.

Operating a power tiller.
◆ Put the tiller in neutral, position it at one corner of the planting area, and set the tines to the correct depth—from 3 inches for heavy, clayey soil to 8 inches for sandy soil.
◆ Start the engine, shift into forward, and guide the machine along one side of the bed. Make a broad turn at the far end, and work back in the opposite direction, creating a U-shaped area of tilled soil.
◆ Continue back and forth until you reach the end, then reverse directions and repeat the pattern in the untilled strips *(inset)*. If your soil is very heavy, set the tines at 6 inches and till again.
◆ Spread the desired amount of organic soil amendments *(Step 2, page 29)* on top of the soil. Set the tines at maximum depth and till in a direction perpendicular to the first set of lines to work in the amendments. If the tiller bucks excessively, go more slowly and raise the tines slightly.

THE COMPOST PILE:
FREE FERTILIZER FROM THROWAWAYS

Making compost is somewhat like setting up a fertilizer factory in your own backyard. The workers in the factory are billions of microorganisms—bacteria and fungi that convert organic waste from your yard and kitchen into a nutrient-rich soil amendment.

A Suitable Container: If organic matter is simply heaped in a pile, the composting process can take up to a year. But if you place the materials in bins that distribute heat and moisture evenly, you will have usable compost in just 3 or 4 weeks. The most efficient composting system uses three bins: one for fresh organic material, one for half-decomposed matter, and one for the finished product. You can buy bins —plastic barrels, for example—or you can make them.

One easy-to-build arrangement is shown below. These bins are 4 feet high and 3 feet square. No floor is necessary. The vertical posts, set into the ground for stability, are 2-by-4s. Grooves cut into the front posts with a router or circular saw allow 1-by-6 slats to slide in and out for easy turning of the compost.

Air circulation around the pile is very important. Here, the front slats are held apart by screws that are driven into one side of the boards. The sides and backs of the bins are heavy-gauge wire screening, held in place by 1-by-6 boards nailed to the top and bottom of the posts.

The Ingredients: To start a compost pile, you need equal proportions of so-called "browns" (shredded sticks, sawdust, and leaves) and "greens" (grass and hedge clippings, garden refuse, and vegetable scraps). Other organic materials, such as wood ashes, fruit peels, crushed eggshells, and coffee grounds, are also helpful. Do not include diseased plants, invasive weeds, pet droppings, or cooked scraps, which will attract vermin.

Place 6 inches of coarse brown material on the bottom. Then add an inch of commercial manure to provide food for the microorganisms, followed by 6 inches of green material, another inch of manure, and an inch of soil. Water until damp, then keep stacking layers in the same sequence and proportions until the bin is full.

Cooking the Pile: Leave the pile alone for a few days, then start turning it with a spading fork several times a week to speed decomposition. After a couple of weeks, shift part of the pile to the next bin, and add fresh kitchen and yard waste to the first; layering does not matter now.

Water both bins occasionally to keep the piles moist. In another 2 weeks, the compost in the second bin should be dark and crumbly; store it in the third bin until ready for use.

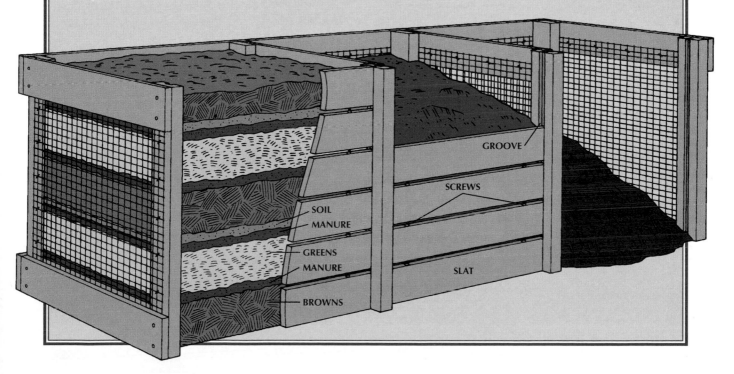

GROOVE

SCREWS

SOIL

MANURE

GREENS

MANURE

SLAT

BROWNS

2

Growing a Blanket of Green

For many, landscaping begins and ends with the lawn—and for good reason. There is no escaping a continuous regimen of lawn upkeep throughout the growing season. A less burdensome alternative is to plant a low-maintenance ground cover such as ivy or periwinkle. Whatever your choice, this chapter holds the keys to a verdant backdrop for your house that will retain its beauty year after year.

Maintaining a Healthy Lawn

Equipment for Mowing and Trimming
Manicuring Your Lawn
Choosing the Right Sprinkler
Applying Fertilizer
Spot Treatments for Isolated Weeds
Spraying Weed-Killer Over a Large Area
Reseeding a Bare Patch
Cutting through Layers of Thatch
Breaking Up Compacted Soil

Growing a New Lawn

Preparing the Bed
New Grass from Seed
Starting a Lawn with Sprigs
Planting with Plugs
Instant Green from Rolls of Sod

A Carpet of Ground Cover

A Technique for Planting
Stabilizing a Slope
Propagation by Cuttings
Multiplication by Division
Controlling the Spread of Ground Covers

An oscillating sprinkler →

Expanses of weed-free, perfectly groomed grass do not occur naturally; they require careful attention and consistent care. Along with the routine demands of mowing and watering, other periodic tasks such as fertilizing, aerating, and dethatching are also necessary to keep the grass green and healthy.

Cutting the Grass: There are a wide variety of mowers available; choose the one that best suits your needs. Sharpen the blade yearly *(page 8)* and keep the lawn free of debris that might dull the blade or be thrown out of the mower's chute. Before starting the engine, adjust the cutting height *(page 36)*. Recommended mowing heights for the most common lawn grasses are given in the chart on pages 112-113.

Lawn clippings can be bagged, but short clippings left on the lawn decompose to a natural fertilizer. Modern mulching mowers, which have a special blade and a fully enclosed deck, chop clippings fine to speed decomposition; you may be able to convert an older mower to work like a mulcher.

For a finished appearance, crop around posts and other hard-to-reach areas with a power trimmer, and use an edger to cut a small, narrow trench along flower beds and sidewalks *(page 37)*.

Providing Water and Food: In summer, when high heat and lower rainfall slow the growth of grass, you will mow your lawn less often but water it more. A thorough watering—perhaps once a week—is preferable to frequent light waterings, which can inhibit the growth of deep roots. Control the amount of water the lawn receives by setting your sprinkler for the correct intensity and area.

Grass does not, of course, live by water alone. To replace soil nutrients, fertilizers must be added. The timing depends on the type of grass, as indicated in the grasses chart. Always sweep excess fertilizer from sidewalks and driveways onto the lawn to prevent runoff into storm drains.

Controlling Weeds: Even in the best-kept lawn, a few weeds are inevitable and must be dug up or destroyed with a selective herbicide that kills weeds without harming grass. Some weed-killers wither parts of the plant they touch. Others are systemic: they are absorbed into the plant, destroying even the roots. Weed-killers can be applied directly to isolated weeds or they can be sprayed over an entire area that is badly infested *(pages 42-43)*.

Most large garden centers carry water-soluble, environmentally safe dyes that when mixed with herbicides in the sprayer help ensure even coverage. Rain or watering soon washes the dye away.

Stimulating Growth: Despite careful watering and fertilizing, a lawn may still deteriorate if thatch—a matted layer of dead grass—becomes too thick, strangling new growth. Strip it off with a thatch rake or a power dethatcher *(page 44);* both devices cut slits through the tightly woven barrier so it can easily be raked away.

The soil in heavily used backyards or play areas can become so compacted that grass roots cannot penetrate it. An aerator *(page 45),* which extracts small plugs of earth to loosen compacted soil, may be needed as often as every 2 years. Periodic aeration also helps prevent thatch buildup.

Compost is an excellent soil amendment, or additive, when raked into the holes left by the aerator. Contact your local extension service to see if composted municipal sludge is available in your area.

> ⚠ *Before repairing or adjusting power lawn-care*
> **CAUTION** *equipment, always unplug an electrically powered machine, or if it has a gasoline engine, disconnect the spark plug wire.*

 TOOLS

Tape measure	Thatch rake or
Screwdriver	power dethatcher
Weeding fork	Grass rake
Spading fork	Aerating fork or
Garden rake	power aerator
Hoe	
Garden trowel	

 **MATERIALS**

Lawn fertilizer	Composted
Grass seed	municipal sludge
Weed-killer	Straw or wood
Stakes	fiber mulch
String	Chain-link fencing
Peat moss	

 SAFETY TIPS

When using lawn-care machinery, wear sturdy leather shoes (preferably steel-tipped), long pants, goggles, and gloves. Also protect your ears when operating loud gasoline-powered machines. Wear gloves when using hand tools to dig or rake.

EQUIPMENT FOR MOWING AND TRIMMING

A reel mower.

The scissoring action of reel blades against a fixed metal bed knife makes a smooth cut, particularly on thin grasses such as bluegrass. Reel mowers are less effective in trimming denser grasses such as zoysia. The blades need frequent sharpening and are easily damaged by twigs or pebbles. In addition to the manual mower shown here, there are also self-propelled power models. Both types are best suited for small, level lawns.

REEL BLADES

ROLLER   BED KNIFE

MULCHING BLADE

The versatile rotary mower.

A walk-behind mower like the one shown above cuts a clean swath through any type of grass and allows you to bag your clippings, discharge them, or mulch them. Similar features are available in riding mowers, which may be worth their extra cost for lawns larger than $\frac{1}{2}$ acre. Essential to mulching is a mulching blade *(photograph),* which is specially curved to lift and slice the grass repeatedly over a long cutting edge.

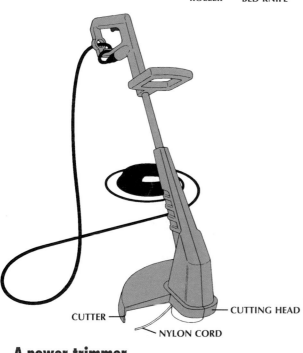

CUTTER   CUTTING HEAD

NYLON CORD

A power trimmer.

Available in gas, plug-in, or battery-powered models, this tool is handy for cropping grass around posts and other obstacles to lawn mowers. A rotating nylon cord lops off grass with a whipping action. Cord frayed through use is replaced from a reel in the cutting head, which when tapped on the ground releases a length of fresh cord. A cutter on the safety guard trims the cord to the correct length.

A power edger.

Trimming along a walk or driveway with an electric or gasoline-powered edger gives a neat, finished look to a lawn. A metal edge guide prevents the machine from wandering while the spinning blade digs a shallow trench along the edge.

BLADE

GUIDE

1. Setting the mower blade height.

◆ Roll the lawn mower onto a driveway or sidewalk and detach the spark plug wire. (Unplug electric models.)

◆ Reach into the discharge chute and rotate the blade so that one end is toward you, then measure the distance from the blade to the ground.

◆ Move the height-adjustment levers *(right)*, raising or lowering the deck to achieve the desired blade height—usually between 1 and 2 inches.

DECK

SPARK PLUG WIRE

HEIGHT-ADJUSTMENT LEVERS

2. Mowing on level lawns and slopes.

On a level lawn, the choice of mowing pattern is up to you. But whether you cut in parallel strips up and down the lawn or in an elongated spiral as shown at left, remember that mowing affects the direction in which grass grows and leans. To prevent stripes in the lawn, change the direction of the pattern each time you mow.

To mow safely on a hillside *(inset),* begin at the top of the slope, and guide a walk-behind power mower across it in parallel lines. With a riding mower, drive up and down the slope for the best stability.

3. Trimming around obstacles.

Hold the power trimmer's cutting head parallel to the ground, an inch or so above the soil, and swing the cutter back and forth in smooth passes, working toward the obstacle.

GUIDE

4. Cutting a clean edge.

For short lengths of edging along sidewalks, driveways, and flower beds, a manual rotary edger may be sufficient, but for bigger jobs, use a power edger *(left)*.

◆ If the blade of your edger is adjustable, set it to the desired depth. Then position the edger so the wheels are on the hard surface.

◆ Turn on the machine and walk at a steady pace, pressing the guide against the edge of the pavement or border.

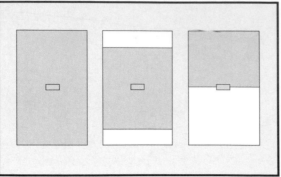

An oscillating sprinkler.

Driven by water pressure from a garden hose, an oscillating sprinkler provides an even dousing of a rectangular area of grass. The perforated, curved crosspiece swings back and forth through all or part of an arc; controls at the base of the crosspiece set the sprinkler to water all of the lawn, the center alone, or either half (*shaded areas, left*).

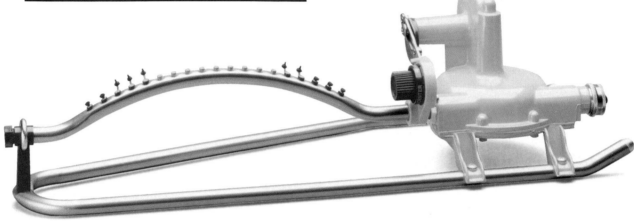

Testing Your Sprinkler Coverage

To check the quantity and distribution of water from your sprinkler, set several shallow containers, such as empty tuna cans, throughout the area to be watered, then run the sprinkler for an hour at the same time of day you water the lawn. You should expect to collect 1 inch of water in an hour, and the amounts of water in each can should be almost equal.

Test for water penetration by pushing a screwdriver tip into the lawn 24 hours after watering it. If you encounter resistance before the tip reaches a depth of 6 inches, water the lawn longer.

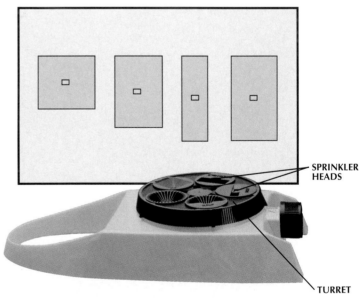

SPRINKLER HEADS

TURRET

A turret sprinkler.

Multiple sprinkler heads on the turret spray rectangular patterns of different lengths and widths. Compared with an oscillator, a turret sprinkler provides a dousing that is quick, heavy, and somewhat uneven.

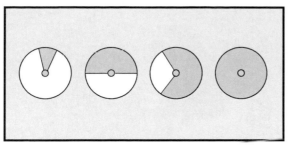

A pulsating sprinkler.
The head of this sprinkler waters grass in a circular pattern that can be adjusted from a narrow wedge to a full circle. The sprinkler head is constantly in motion to prevent water from pooling, and the stream can be varied from a fine spray for small areas to a heavy, longer-range jet.

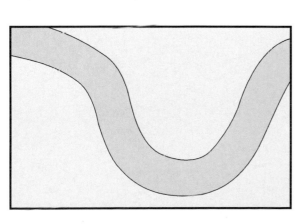

A traveling sprinkler.
This self-propelled sprinkler is ideal for long, narrow lawns. Using its own hose as a track, it creeps along the route even uphill, while the spinning nozzles soak the grass. The traveling sprinkler shown here drags its hose behind it; other models reel in the slack hose as they move across the grass.

A sprinkler hose.
Tiny holes along the top of the hose provide a fine, soaking mist. The flexible hose is especially suited for very narrow areas. It can also be laid to match an irregular plot's contours (left).

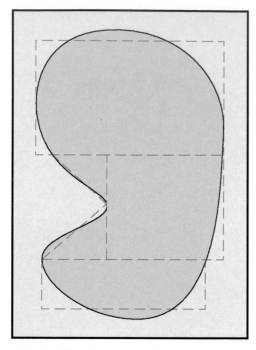

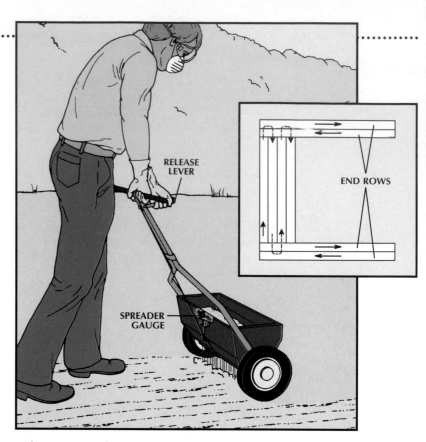

Calculating the quantity.

◆ To determine how much fertilizer you need for your lawn, divide the grassy area into rough geometric shapes such as rectangles, circles, and triangles *(above)*.
◆ Calculate the area of each section, then add those figures together. Small areas outside the lawn that happen to be included in this estimate tend to compensate for grassy patches that are left out.

Using a trough spreader.

◆ Set the spreader gauge according to the instructions on the fertilizer package.
◆ At a corner of the lawn, open the trough with the release lever and immediately start walking at an even, moderate pace along one side of the lawn. Close the trough when you reach the far end to avoid burning the grass with excess fertilizer.
◆ Turn the spreader around and position it so that the next row touches but does not overlap the first. Open the trough and run the second row, then make two similar rows at the opposite end of the lawn *(inset)*.
◆ Fill in the remaining area by running rows perpendicular to the end rows, being careful not to overlap the fertilizer at any point.

What to Look for in a Fertilizer

Lawn fertilizers come in liquid, pellet, and granular form, with labels that rate the nitrogen, phosphorus, and potassium content according to a three-number code. For example, one common rating, 10-6-4, indicates that 10 percent of the fertilizer bulk is nitrogen, 6 percent phosphorus, and 4 percent potassium. Make a soil test *(page 29)* annually to check for deficiency in any of these three minerals. If the soil is found wanting in one of them, use fertilizer with a higher proportion of the mineral in short supply.

Liquid fertilizer is easy to apply, but the nutrients leach through the soil quickly, necessitating frequent reapplication. Although time-release pellets last 6 months or more, they are costly and slow acting. The more common choice is dry granular fertilizer because it is quick, reliable, and relatively inexpensive.

Using a broadcast spreader.
◆ Calibrate the spreader according to the fertilizer directions, then, beginning at a corner of the lawn, push the spreader at a steady pace that scatters fertilizer 3 or 4 feet to each side.
◆ Work up and down the lawn in wide parallel sweeps. To ensure full coverage near the edges of the path where the fertilizer falls less densely, overlap the rows by about 1 foot. Approach corners and boundaries close enough to give them full coverage.
◆ Repeat the pattern at a right angle to the original rows *(inset)*.

> ### ⚠ CAUTION
> *Fertilizers, weed-killers, and other chemicals can be harmful if they come in contact with the skin. Read the labels carefully and follow their recommendations. In addition to long pants and a long-sleeved shirt, it is advisable to wear rubber gloves and eye protection. A dust mask traps particles of dry fertilizers.*

SPOT TREATMENTS FOR ISOLATED WEEDS

A weeding fork.
◆ If the soil around the weed is hard, soften it by watering over a period of days.
◆ Grasp the runners or leaves in one hand; with the other, push a weeding fork 3 or 4 inches into the earth alongside the main root. For an unusually stubborn weed, dig the fork all the way around it, trying not to tear the leaves or break the roots.
◆ Lever the fork in the surrounding soil to work the roots free, then pull up lightly on the bunched leaves to remove the weed with its roots intact.
◆ Sprinkle a few grass seeds in the hole that has been left by the weed.

A trigger sprayer.
◆ Hold the bottle of weed-killer above the weed, and spray directly onto the center of the plant, coating the leaves and main stem.
◆ Allow 2 to 4 weeks for the weed to shrivel and die, then remove it.

SPRAYING WEED-KILLER OVER A LARGE AREA

Using a pressurized sprayer.
◆ Along one end of the weed-infested area, mark off a 3-yard strip with a pair of staked parallel strings.
◆ Build up pressure in the sprayer with a few strokes of the hand pump, then spray the area between the strings, holding the wand about 12 inches above the lawn and moving it quickly and steadily for a light, even coverage.
◆ Move one of the strings to mark off an adjoining strip, and treat this area in the same way.
◆ Continue spraying strips until you have covered the entire area.

Using a garden-hose sprayer.

◆ Read the weed-killer's label to see how many square feet one jarful will cover, mark off that area with string and stakes, then run a string down the middle to divide it in half.

◆ Fill the sprayer jar with the weed-killer-and-water mixture specified in the label instructions; then screw the sprayer nozzle onto a garden hose and attach the jar to the nozzle.

◆ Turn on the hose and start the flow of weed-killer by covering the air-siphon hole with your thumb or by depressing the trigger, depending on your model.

◆ Spray half the weed-killer evenly on one side of the string, then apply the remainder on the other side.

RESEEDING A BARE PATCH

1. Preparing the soil.

◆ Turn the soil in the plot with a spading fork, digging 5 or 6 inches deep.

◆ Remove 3 inches of soil and work the remainder to break up clods.

◆ Dust the area lightly with lawn fertilizer and add a 3-inch layer of composted municipal sludge or peat moss, then use the spading fork to mix it thoroughly with the underlying soil.

◆ Make the soil even with the surrounding earth by tamping it down with your foot. If necessary, adjust the soil level, either by removing mix or by adding and tamping down more made from the 3 inches of soil removed from the area.

◆ Smooth the surface of the soil with the back of a garden rake.

2. Reseeding the patch.

◆ With your thumb and forefinger, sprinkle grass seeds $\frac{1}{8}$ inch apart over the patch (right).

◆ Work the seeds into the top $\frac{1}{8}$ inch of soil mix with a garden rake, then tamp the soil lightly with the back of a hoe.

◆ Cover the patch with a thin layer of straw—half the soil should show through—to protect the seeds from birds and wind, and lightly mist the area with a garden hose.

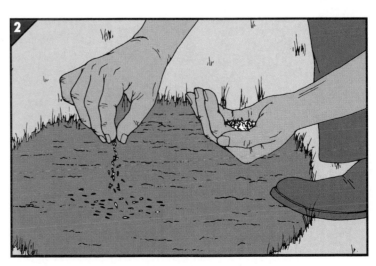

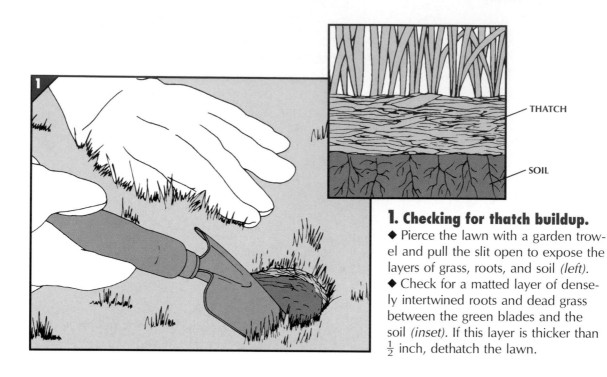

THATCH

SOIL

1. Checking for thatch buildup.
◆ Pierce the lawn with a garden trowel and pull the slit open to expose the layers of grass, roots, and soil *(left)*.
◆ Check for a matted layer of densely intertwined roots and dead grass between the green blades and the soil *(inset)*. If this layer is thicker than $\frac{1}{2}$ inch, dethatch the lawn.

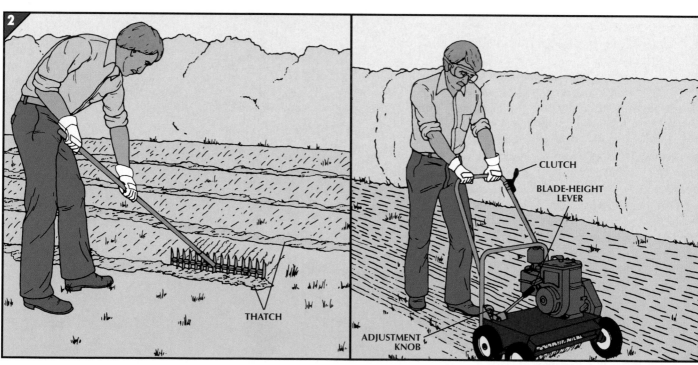

THATCH

CLUTCH

BLADE-HEIGHT LEVER

ADJUSTMENT KNOB

2. Dethatching the lawn.
For a small plot, work in rows about 2 feet wide with a thatch rake *(above, left)*. Hold the rake at a 30-degree angle and press the teeth through the thatch. Pull the rake through the grass to dislodge the thatch.

◆ For large areas, rent a self-propelled power dethatcher *(above, right)*. At the center of the lawn, pull the height lever to lower the blades into the thatch, then turn the adjustment knob until the blades barely penetrate the soil.
◆ Engage the clutch, then run the ma-

chine over the lawn. Follow the pattern used for mowing *(page 36)*, but do not overlap the rows.
◆ Remove the thatch with a flexible grass rake.

BREAKING UP COMPACTED SOIL

1. Aerating the lawn.

◆ Mow the lawn and saturate the ground with a sprinkler a day in advance of when you plan to aerate.

◆ For a small lawn, thrust an aerating fork with three or four tines *(below, left)* into the ground at 6-inch intervals; try to penetrate to a depth of at least 3 inches. If the soil is too compacted, make a shallower pass,

resoak the lawn, and try again.

◆ Work along one boundary, and then back and forth parallel to this line, leaving the extracted cores scattered on the ground.

For large areas, rent a power aerator *(below, right).*

◆ Beginning at the center of the lawn, start the aerator's engine and warm it

up with the clutch disengaged.

◆ Engage the clutch to start the corer drum, and guide the aerator in the pattern that is used for mowing, but do not overlap rows.

◆ In particularly hard soil you may need to increase penetration either by adding water to the corer drum or by attaching weights, if they were provided, or both.

CLUTCH LEVER

CORER DRUM

2. Crumbling the cores.

For a small area, use the back of a garden rake to break up the cores *(left)* and spread a $\frac{1}{2}$-inch layer of composted municipal sludge or other soil amendment over the area, filling the core holes. Water the lawn thoroughly.

For larger lawns, drag a section of chain-link fencing across the lawn—either by hand or attached to a lawn tractor—to break up the cores.

Whether establishing a new lawn on an empty lot or replacing an old one that is terminally choked with weeds, you must start the job from scratch. Although not complicated, the process requires careful planning and hard work.

Choosing the Right Grass: The type of grass you plant depends largely upon the local climate. Cool-season grasses, so called because they grow rapidly in the cool temperatures of spring and autumn while languishing in the warm months of a relatively short summer, do well in northern climates. Warm-season grasses, which are more suited to southern climates, flourish in the heat of a long summer and are dormant in cool months. In regions with wide variations of temperature, a mixture of grasses gives the best results.

Check the grass chart on pages 112 and 113 for other characteristics such as color, texture, and drought tolerance that you should consider when choosing a grass.

Selecting a Planting Method: How you plant your new lawn depends primarily upon the kind of grass you plan to grow and on how quickly you want the lawn to be established.

Seeding *(right)* is the least expensive way to start a lawn and offers the greatest choice of grasses. It is also the slowest because the plants must sprout before they can begin to spread and fill in the lawn. Planting alternatives for warm-season grasses and for sterile hybrids, which produce no seeds, are sprigging *(page 48)* and plugging *(page 49)*. Sprigs and plugs generally fill in faster than a seeded lawn and, in the meantime, are less fragile. In both cases, the sparsely planted mature plants send out new shoots that fill the gaps in between.

The quickest—and most expensive—way to a new lawn is sodding, in which long strips of fully developed turf are set on bare ground *(page 50)*. Lay sod within 36 hours of its harvest, and have your plot ready before the delivery date. For large lawns, consider having the sod delivered in installments so it does not dry out before planting.

Preparing the Site: No matter which planting method you choose, you must carefully prepare the planting bed *(below)*. Before replacing a weed-infested lawn, apply a systemic herbicide formulated to kill all plant life. Follow the manufacturer's instructions, allowing the chemical to dissipate before replanting. Use a sod cutter to remove the old turf, and prepare and smooth the bed *(below and at right)*.

 **TOOLS**

Sod cutter
Tiller
Garden rake
Lawn roller
Hopper
Mechanical spreader
Grass rake
Garden hoe
Grass plugger
Tamper

 **MATERIALS**

Straw
$3\frac{1}{2}$-inch nails
2-by-4, 8 feet long
2-by-2, 6 feet long
Two 1-by-2s, 3 feet long

PREPARING THE BED

1. Smoothing the soil.
◆ Till the lawn bed, then rake it, removing stones and other debris.
◆ Check the grading and drainage around the house *(pages 22-23)* and in the rest of the yard *(pages 18-21)*, and make corrections if necessary.
◆ Test the soil and add amendments as needed *(pages 28-30)*; work them into the soil thoroughly.
◆ Rake the soil again to remove any remaining debris.

2. Firming the soil.

◆ Remove the filler plug on the barrel of a lawn roller and fill the barrel halfway with water in order to increase the roller's weight.

◆ Push the roller in parallel rows across the lawn bed to flatten it, then roll the area again, perpendicular to the first pass.

◆ Fill in any low spots revealed by rolling, rake the fill smooth, then roll the entire bed again.

FILLER PLUG

NEW GRASS FROM SEED

1. Sowing seed with a hopper.

◆ Measure the correct quantity of seed for the entire area *(chart, pages 112-113)*, then divide it into two equal portions. Do not try to speed growth by using more than the recommended quantity of seed.

◆ Walk slowly over the plot in parallel lines, scattering seed from the hopper by turning the crank steadily until you have covered the entire area once with half the seed; then, walking in rows at right angles to the first direction, sow the other half of the seed. For even coverage over a large area, use a mechanical spreader *(pages 40-41)*, following the same sowing pattern.

◆ Rake the area lightly with a grass rake to mix the seed into the soil, then roll it with a half-filled roller to ensure good contact between the seed and soil.

2. Covering and watering.

◆ Scatter clean straw over the seedbed, covering it so that half the soil can be seen beneath the straw.

◆ Mist the bed just enough to soak the soil without forming puddles or rivulets.

◆ Keep the soil dark with moisture until the seeds germinate—about 2 to 3 weeks, depending on the type of grass and the growing conditions—then water once a day until the seedlings are $\frac{1}{2}$ inch tall. Thereafter, water as frequently as necessary to prevent the lawn from drying out.

◆ Do not mow or walk on the new grass until it is 3 inches high; at that point, either rake off the straw or leave it to decompose into the soil.

STARTING A LAWN WITH SPRIGS

1. Furrowing the soil.

◆ After preparing the bed *(pages 46-47),* soak it with water and let it seep in for 24 hours.

◆ With the corner of a garden-hoe blade, cut a series of straight furrows 3 to 4 inches deep and 6 to 12 inches apart.

GRASS SPRIG

2. Setting the sprigs.

◆ Place sprigs in each furrow at 6- to 12-inch intervals, slanting them upward from the bottom of a furrow to the top of one side *(right).* The closer they are planted, the faster the lawn will fill in.

◆ Press soil gently around the roots with your hands, leaving some blades of each sprig protruding above the ground.

◆ Smooth the soil and level it around the sprigs.

◆ When you have planted all of the sprigs, keep the lawn moist until they have rooted, then water them as you would a mature lawn.

PLANTING WITH PLUGS

1. Cutting holes for planting.

◆ Prepare the soil bed *(pages 46-47)*, soak it thoroughly, and let the water seep in for 24 hours before planting.

◆ Mark the placement of each plug hole, spacing them as recommended for your grass type.

◆ Use a grass plugger, available at a nursery or garden center, to make the holes. Press the foot bar down until it touches the ground, then twist the handle a quarter-turn. Lift the plugger, extracting a core of soil, then deposit the core on the ground.

TRICKS OF THE TRADE

A Spacing Tool for Plugs

Grass plugs should be planted in even rows 12 to 18 inches apart. You can mark a precise planting grid on your lot with the homemade spacing tool shown above. To make one, drive $3\frac{1}{2}$-inch nails through a 2-by-4 at whatever interval you have chosen, then attach a 6-foot-long 2-by-2, braced with two 3-foot-long 1-by-2s, to serve as a handle. Drag the tool the length of the plot to scratch parallel lines in the soil; pull it across the plot to complete the grid. Plant a plug at each intersection.

2. Planting the plugs.

◆ Fill the holes with water; allow it to drain completely.

◆ If your plugs are square *(photograph)*, round them gently with your hands to fit the holes. Then insert one plug in each hole.

◆ With the ball of your foot, step gently on each plug to bring it even with the surrounding soil.

◆ Break up the extracted soil cores with a garden rake. Using a grass rake, smooth the ground between plugs, erasing any footprints.

◆ Water the area daily for 2 weeks, then water every other day for a month until the plugs have rooted.

◆ Once the plugs are established, water and mow the lawn regularly to stimulate growth.

GRASS PLUG

1. Laying the sod.

◆ Prepare the bed as directed on pages 46 and 47, making it 1 inch lower than any adjoining walkways, driveways, or patios.

◆ Wet the soil thoroughly a day or 2 before laying the sod, and keep the soil bed moist but not muddy while laying the rolls.

◆ Lay the first course of sod along a straight pavement or a staked string to provide a uniform edge. Unroll sod gently to avoid breaking off corners and edges. If a section feels uneven, roll it up and relevel the ground beneath it.

◆ For later courses, kneel on a piece of plywood or planking laid across the new sod to avoid creating depressions. Butt the sod rolls together as tightly as possible, staggering joints between them as shown above.

◆ At the end of a row, cut excess with a sharp knife *(inset),* and use these pieces to fill oddly shaped areas around the perimeter of your lot.

2. Establishing root contact.

◆ Tamp the sod firmly against the soil bed; alternatively, roll the turf with an empty lawn roller.

◆ Water the new sod every day for 2 weeks; small pieces at the ends of rows may dry out more quickly than full sections and need more frequent watering. After 2 weeks, try to lift a piece of sod by the grass blades; if it has rooted, the blades will tear and you can begin watering less frequently. Otherwise, retamp the piece, continue watering daily, and test again in a few more days.

A Carpet of Ground Cover

Ground covers are excellent problem solvers. Many flourish in deep shade where grasses won't grow. Their wide range of color, foliage, and flowers can break up the monotony of open spaces or form a transition between low grasses and tall shrubs. And planting a hillside with ground cover eliminates the hazards of mowing on a slope, yet still prevents erosion.

Planting: Some ground covers can be grown from seed, but most are propagated either as cuttings taken from established plants or by dividing large plants into smaller ones, as described on pages 53-55. You can use these methods yourself if you have access to a patch of ground cover either in your own yard or that of a cooperative neighbor. Alternatively, ground covers are sold as immature plants in lots of 50 or more temporarily rooted in a shallow tray called a flat.

The chart on pages 114-115 provides a selection of ground cover plants including information on their special requirements. Consult your nursery about the number of plants of a particular variety you will need to cover a given area. And before planting, mulch the area with a layer of shredded pine bark to help keep weeds at bay. Even so, expect to weed often during the first year.

Coping with Slopes: To prevent the rain from washing newly planted ground cover down an erosion-prone slope, you must stabilize the soil long enough for the ground cover to spread out. Jute netting, a loosely woven, biodegradable material, works especially well *(page 53)*. It does not restrict plant growth or prevent water and nutrients from reaching the roots. Within 6 to 9 months the netting starts to disintegrate, disappearing completely in about 2 years.

Controlling Expansion: After ground covers have become established, they may run rampant. Keep varieties that spread by surface runners in check by pruning. Cut the runner with pruning shears no closer than three or four nodes —points where leaves attach to the stem—from the main stem. A species that widens its coverage by means of the root system can be temporarily contained by cutting the roots along the border of the bed *(page 55)*, but for a more permanent solution, install edging *(page 86)*. Whenever ground cover begins to pop up in a lawn or flower bed, weed it out immediately before it grows beyond control.

TOOLS

Garden trowel
Hammer
3-inch masonry trowel
Hand fork
Spade
Weeding fork

MATERIALS

Mulch
Jute netting
Sod staples
Flat
Plant hormone powder
Rooting medium
Sheet of glass or clear plastic

A TECHNIQUE FOR PLANTING

1. Separating the plants.
◆ Remove no more than half a dozen plants and rooting medium from the flat. Separate the plants with your fingers *(above)*, taking care not to injure the roots.
◆ Set the plants in the ground immediately *(overleaf)*.

2. Setting the plants.

◆ To prepare a planting hole, push a garden trowel through the mulch and into the soil, then pull it toward you, opening a small pocket in the ground.

◆ Holding the soil back with the trowel, set a plant in the pocket, with about $\frac{1}{4}$ inch of its stem below ground level *(left)*.

◆ With the trowel, gently push the displaced soil back into the pocket.

3. Tamping the soil.

◆ Smooth the soil and mulch with your fingers, patting the mulch down around the stem, forming a slight depression to catch and hold moisture *(inset)*.

◆ Set in the remaining plants, and water them for at least half an hour with a lawn sprinkler or with a hose set for a fine mist. Continue to water the new plants every other day for a month.

STABILIZING A SLOPE

SOD STAPLE

Bracing plants with jute netting.
◆ Strip away any sod, grade the slope if necessary *(pages 20-21)*, and prepare the soil for planting *(pages 28-30)*.
◆ Working uphill from the bottom of the slope, unroll strips of jute netting *(photograph)* across the incline. Overlap the strips 8 inches and secure them with sod staples *(above)*. Cover the area with an inch of mulch.
◆ With a 3-inch masonry trowel, dig holes for the plants, in staggered rows to prevent water from washing straight down the hill.
◆ After setting the plants, mold a basin around the lower side of each stem with your hand to prevent runoff. Then water as described on page 52, Step 3.

PROPAGATION BY CUTTINGS

1. Obtaining a cutting.
◆ Cut a 3- to 6-inch length from a main stem or an entire side stem of a well-established plant. The stem should contain three to five nodes.
◆ With a small sharp knife, make a clean, slanting cut slightly below the nodes *(right)*.

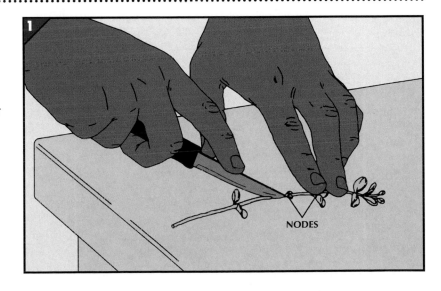

NODES

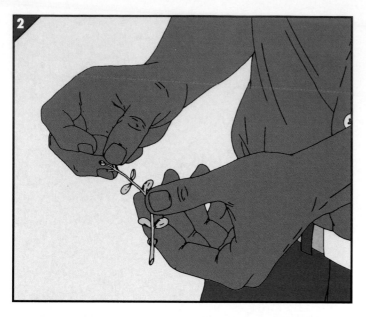

2. Preparing the cutting for planting.

◆ Pinch off any flowers or seed heads from the stem *(left)*; if allowed to remain, they will divert nutrients away from the roots that will form on the cutting.

◆ Trim the leaves from the bottom of the cutting so that no foliage will be buried in the planting.

◆ Allow the cut end of the stem to dry out slightly; if the leaves begin to wilt, place them on a damp towel.

3. Planting the cuttings.

◆ Fill a flat with a moistened rooting medium, such as a combination of sand and peat moss in equal parts, to about an inch from the top.

◆ With a stick or a pencil, poke holes in the medium just deep enough to cover two or three nodes on the cuttings.

◆ Dip the end of each cutting into plant hormone powder, available at nurseries or garden-supply outlets, to encourage root growth. Set the cutting in a hole and tamp rooting medium down around it.

◆ After planting all the cuttings, water the entire flat gently but thoroughly.

◆ Cover the flat with a sheet of glass or clear plastic to protect the young plants until they can survive outdoors.

◆ Keep them in a warm room and out of direct sunlight. When new leaves appear, the cuttings are ready to be transplanted *(page 52)*.

MULTIPLICATION BY DIVISION

1. Uprooting the plants.

◆ Water the plants well a couple of days before you divide them to soften the ground.

◆ Using a hand fork or a spading fork, dig around a clump of plants containing 8 to 12 new plants.

◆ Raise the clump and guide the roots away from the fork with your free hand *(right)*.

2. Separating the plants.

◆ Shake or rinse enough soil from the clump to reveal the roots, then carefully pull apart individual plants *(left)*.

◆ After discarding any wilted or yellowed plants, return two or three of the stems to the original hole, then set the rest in a new hole and water them thoroughly.

CONTROLLING THE SPREAD OF GROUND COVERS

Countering an invasion.

For deep-rooting plants—pachysandra and ivy, for example—slice straight down into the soil along the edge of the ground cover bed with a sharp spade, penetrating to the full depth of the plants' roots, usually about 6 to 8 inches *(right)*.

If ground cover begins to pop up in a lawn or flower bed, remove it by hand with a weeding fork. Hold the base of the ground cover with one hand as you push the blade down into the soil alongside the root *(far right)*, then lever the plant out of the ground.

3 Shrubs and Trees

Shrubs and their larger cousins, trees, create a variety of visual delights, but they have practical uses, too. Trees can shade a deck or patio; shrubs can serve as a living privacy fence, a border to walkways and flower beds, or a windscreen. Planting—or transplanting—shrubs and trees is not difficult, and with regular pruning and fertilizing, these stately specimens will provide a lifetime of enjoyment.

Shrubs: Beautiful and Versatile

Shrubs are surely the most versatile of landscape elements. With a little training or trimming, they can add a variety of shapes and textures to the yard *(below)*.

Basic Shrub Care: Throughout the spring and summer, give shrubs a long, slow watering every 2 weeks —every 7 to 10 days during dry spells. Fertilize them no later than the spring growth spurt; later applications stimulate new growth that will suffer in winter.

Spread shredded pine bark or other organic mulch around shrubs to insulate the roots against heat and cold, and to inhibit weeds. Renew mulch in the spring and fall.

The Value of Pruning: Few tasks are more important than pruning. It eliminates damaged and diseased wood as well as crossing branches, which can abrade each other and leave the plant open to infection. Pruning also encourages new growth and boosts flower and fruit production. Finally, pruning keeps the shrub in bounds and shapes it.

Prune shrubs several times a year. In the spring, remove winter damage and do light trimming. Wait to prune shrubs such as azaleas, which flower on old wood, until the blossoms have wilted. Most other shrubs can be pruned through the winter and up to midspring— or in summer after flowering.

Summer calls for biweekly shapings and trimmings. After the shrubs have flowered, snip off one third of the older stems at ground level, so that each plant renews itself every 3 years or so.

Winterizing: Some shrubs need protection from wind, cold, and snow. A local nursery can tell you which plants need help through the winter. Effective methods of protecting shrubs are shown on page 63. For the best results, winterize shrubs before the first hard freeze.

Heavy, wet snow is especially damaging to evergreens. After a storm, dislodge snow gently, taking care not to snap the branches.

TOOLS

Pruning shears
Loppers
Pruning saw
Hedge trimmer
Hedge shears
Action hoe
Sprinkler extension
Sprinkler hose
Staple gun
Saw
Hammer

MATERIALS

Mulch
Fertilizer
Burlap
Twine
2-by-3s
1-by-4s
3-inch nails
Stakes and string

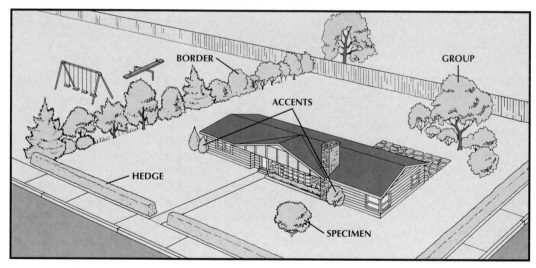

Using shrubs in a landscape.
Depending on where they are planted and how they are combined, shrubs offer many landscaping options. Besides their visual appeal, shrubs can be living fences or screens for trash bins and compost heaps. In deciding what shrubs to plant and where, consider how they will look in relation to the house, as well as how they appear from indoors. Landscape architects call a single free-standing shrub selected for its color, shape, or seasonal blossoms a specimen. Several shrubs differing in sizes and colors, perhaps combined with a tree, are known as a group. Shrubs strategically located to contrast with or complement an architectural feature are called accents. A closely spaced row of a single species forms a hedge, useful to define property lines and preserve privacy. A combination of trees and shrubs becomes an informal border, offering diverse and contrasting colors and textures.

Pruning to promote growth.

◆ To encourage a new branch *(dashed lines)* in a sparse area of a shrub, grasp a branch just below a lateral bud—that is, a bud pointing outward from the side of the branch.

◆ Hold a pair of pruning shears at a 45-degree angle and sever the branch about $\frac{1}{4}$ inch above the bud, taking care not to damage it *(inset).*

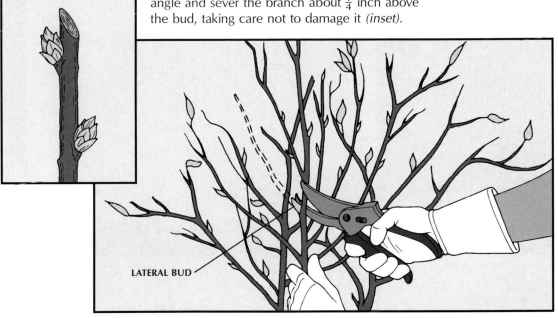

LATERAL BUD

Removing damaged wood.

◆ Cut back a broken or diseased branch to healthy wood, either at a point just beyond a lateral bud or flush with the nearest healthy stem *(left).*

◆ After cutting branches from a diseased shrub, clean blades of shears or saw with alcohol to avoid infecting other plants.

Thinning for health and light.
◆ After the growing season each year, trim and shape the shrub's outer branches. Remove completely any branches that are weak or misshapen, or that cross other branches. Prune individual branches at a main stem, and main stems near the ground *(right)*.

◆ Then, to let sunlight reach new buds and foliage next spring, cut away up to one third of the oldest stems.

The right way to prune roses.
◆ Every fall—after the last bloom but well before the first frost—cut away deadwood, small shoots, and crossing branches. Then cut back every main branch by a third of its length *(above, left)*.

◆ In the spring, cut away any stems damaged by winter weather. Then prune all healthy branches back to the point where their stems are at least

$\frac{3}{8}$ inch thick *(above, right)*. The spring pruning should leave a compact, bowl-shaped bush.

◆ During the growing season, regularly trim away all dead and damaged wood, as well as small branches.

Trimming hedges.

For a formal hedge, stretch a level string taut between posts at the ends of the hedge as a cutting guide. To speed the work, use an electric or battery-operated hedge trimmer held at the height of the string. Draw the trimmer across the hedge top, taking care not to poke the tip of the tool into the hedge. Alternatively, use hedge shears as shown in the inset. If any long shoots are growing into a gap in the hedge, cut the shoots back with pruning shears to stimulate thick growth that will fill the hole.

Shape an informal, relatively irregular hedge as you would a shrub, using pruning shears and trying to create a natural, feathery appearance; take special care to prune out any branches that have grown faster than the others.

Trim both formal and informal hedges narrower at the top than at the bottom, to permit sunlight to reach the base of the hedge. After trimming a hedge, shake it to dislodge the clippings, then rake them away.

ROUTINE CARE TO KEEP SHRUBS HEALTHY

Stirring up the soil.

Cultivating the soil around a shrub bed makes weeding easier and watering more effective. Use an action hoe *(left)* to loosen weeds and break up compacted soil.

◆ Push the hoe blade about 2 inches into the earth—shallower if it catches the roots of a shrub—and work it back and forth parallel to the surface.

◆ After weeding the bed, use the hoe again to smooth the soil before watering or applying mulch.

Getting water to the roots.

The best way to water specimens and small groups is with a sprinkler extension *(above, left)*. This wandlike device with a fine-spray nozzle allows you to direct water at the base of a shrub. For larger groups and hedges, surround the bed with a sprinkler hose *(above, right)*. Water shrubs for at least 10 minutes or until the soil is thoroughly saturated. Puddles on the ground indicate overwatering, which can damage the roots; stop watering immediately.

Spreading mulch.

Twice a year, rake away old mulch from around shrubs and replace it with fresh material. In spring, spread an even layer of dense material, such as woodchips or ground-up bark, about 2 inches thick. Use only aged mulch—new chips and bark leach valuable nitrogen from the soil—and keep it away from stems; moisture in the mulch could encourage fungus, insect infestation, and root rot.

Before the first frost, insulate the bed with 3 inches of pine needles or oak leaves.

COUNTERMEASURES AGAINST THE COLD

Protection from wind and snow.

Before the first frost, cover low-growing shrubs with ever-green branches *(below, left)* or spread a double thickness of burlap over them and peg it to the ground.

To shield taller shrubs that are exposed to the full force of the wind, build a shelter of stakes and burlap to the full height of the shrub *(center)*. First, drive several stakes in a tight circle all around the plant, then staple the burlap to the stakes.

Wind twine around evergreens to prevent heavy, wet snow from weighing down the branches and breaking them. Loop the twine around the bottom of the shrub, then wrap it tightly enough to hold the branches upright *(right)*. At the top, tie the twine into another loop.

CROSSBAR

Shelter under an eave.

A sloping shelter on a frame of 2-by-3s prevents snow that slides off a roof from damaging shrubs next to a house.

◆ Cut a pair of pointed 2-by-3 posts at least 2 feet longer than the height of the shrubs and drive them a foot or more into the ground next to the house. In front of the shrubs, drive posts 1 foot shorter than the posts erected next to the wall.

◆ Fasten 2-by-3 crossbars to each pair of posts, then nail a canopy of 1-by-4s on the crossbars as shown at left.

Often, as a landscaping plan evolves and matures, the need to discard or transplant old shrubs and to plant new ones arises. Techniques for accomplishing these tasks are shown on these and the following pages.

Timing and Preparation: Moving an old shrub—or planting a new one—is best done in early spring or fall. A few days before transplanting a shrub, water it generously to soften the soil around its roots, then proceed as shown on the next page. Have a tarpaulin on hand to help move the shrub easily, and plastic sheeting to keep soil off the lawn.

Buying from a Nursery: Except for some flowering shrubs—rhodo-

dendron and laurel, for example—which can be propagated through a technique called layering *(page 69)*—new shrubs come most often from nurseries. The plants come in three forms: rooted in a ball of soil and wrapped in burlap; grown and rooted in plastic containers; and with bare roots.

Selecting Healthy Plants: Choose shrubs suited to your climate and soil conditions *(pages 120-123)* and check their condition carefully. Sound, undamaged bark and bright foliage on well-shaped branches spaced evenly around the stem are signs of a hardy specimen. Reject plants that have broken branches, bruised bark, or pale leaves, or

those that are growing in dry soil.

Ask a nursery worker to show you the roots of container-grown plants. Look for a thick profusion of roots at the rootball's bottom; reject a shrub with roots that coil around the rootball or protrude from the top—sure signs of being potbound. In a healthy burlapped shrub, the rootball has a firm, solid feeling, with moist soil and no weeds. Bare-root stock should be undamaged, clean smelling, and uniform in color.

Plant shrubs immediately if possible, or store them in shade and keep the roots moist; if you cannot plant a bare-rooted shrub within a week, bury it in a shallow trench and keep it watered until you can plant it permanently.

 **TOOLS**

 **MATERIALS**

 **SAFETY TIPS**

Tools		Materials	
Pruning shears	Digging bar	Plastic sheeting	Peat moss
Mattock	Garden fork	Twine	Sand
Spade	Garden trowel	Tarpaulin	Fertilizer
		Burlap	Rooting powder

Shrubs are heavy; lift with the arms and legs and wear a back brace to reduce risk of back strain. Gloves protect your hands during spade work.

DISCARDING AN UNWANTED PLANT

1. Digging out the roots.
◆ Cut off most of the shrub's outer branches with pruning shears and trim main stems to a length of 2 or 3 feet.
◆ With a mattock, dig a trench around the shrub 1 foot or more from the stem and extending down through the root system.
◆ Undercut the shrub with a spade or digging bar to sever all the roots, then pull out the shrub by the trunk.

2. Refilling the hole.

◆ Knock the soil off the roots and into the hole with a spade or garden fork. If the plant is diseased, spread plastic sheeting in the hole to collect the soil and dispose of it away from the yard and garden.

◆ Refill the hole with soil and tamp it firmly. Add more soil to form a loose mound 4 to 6 inches high; the soil will settle in a few months, leaving the area level.

RELOCATING A SHRUB

1. Defining the rootball.

◆ Wrap the plant with twine to gather the branches into a compact bundle.

◆ Score the ground with the point of a shovel or spade to mark a circle roughly the diameter of the wrapped plant; this defines the size of the rootball. Make another circle about 9 inches outside the first.

2. Cutting out the rootball.

◆ Lay a canvas tarpaulin or sheet of heavy plastic next to the outside circle to receive the soil.

◆ Dig out the soil between the two circles to the depth of the shrub's main roots, usually about 18 inches. Undercut the rootball all around the plant with the spade or shovel, freeing it.

3. Wrapping the rootball.

◆ Cut a square sheet of natural-fiber, biodegradable burlap about 3 times the diameter of the rootball and place it next to the hole; do not use synthetic fabric or plastic.

◆ Push against one side of the rootball to tip the shrub on its side and stuff at least half of the burlap under the tilted rootball *(left, top)*. For large shrubs, consider enlisting a helper.

◆ Tip the ball toward the opposite side of the hole, then pull the burlap from under the ball *(left, bottom)*, roughly centering the ball on the burlap square. Lift the edges of the burlap and tie them securely around the stem with twine.

4. Pulling out the shrub.

◆ Set a sheet of canvas or heavy plastic next to the hole and lift the shrub onto the sheet. You may need a helper to assist in moving medium-sized or larger shrubs.

◆ Carry or slide the shrub on the sheet to its new location. Before replanting, unwrap the branches but leave the rootball in the burlap. Cut away any broken branches and prune the shrub by about a third to compensate for any roots lost through digging it up.

◆ Refill the old hole with soil.

PLANTING A BALLED AND BURLAPPED SHRUB

1. Digging the hole.
At the new location, dig a circular hole about twice as wide and half again as deep as the rootball. Pile the soil on a plastic or canvas sheet next to the hole.

2. Conditioning the soil.
Add peat moss and other amendments to the soil that was removed. Blend the soil and other materials thoroughly, keeping the mixture on the sheet and off grass or ground cover.

Soil recipes: For loamy soil, add one part peat moss to two parts soil; for clay soil, add one part peat moss and one part sand to one part soil. For sandy soil, mix equal amounts of peat moss and soil. To any of these mixtures, add slow-release fertilizer in the amount recommended on the package.

3. Making a base for the shrub.
Shovel a layer of the conditioned soil into the hole and compact it with your feet or a tamper. Repeat the process, partially filling the hole to a depth about 2 inches shallower than the height of the rootball.

4. Positioning the shrub.

◆ Set the shrub in the hole, adjusting the bottom as needed to make the main stem vertical. Lay a straight stick across the hole to make sure the top of the rootball is about 2 inches above ground level. If the shrub sits too high or too low, lift it out of the hole and add or remove conditioned soil to bring the shrub to the right height.

◆ Add soil mixture to the hole around the rootball, tamping as you go, until the hole is two-thirds full. Then loosen the burlap and spread it over the soil mixture *(inset)*.

◆ Fill the hole with water, and let it seep into the ground. Then add soil mixture to about 1 inch above ground level and tamp it down firmly.

5. Forming a basin of soil.

◆ Build a soil dam about 4 inches high around the planting hole to catch water for the shrub. Fill this basin with water and let it seep into the soil.

◆ Spread a 2-inch layer of mulch or bark chips around the shrub. Cover the basin walls but stop 2 inches short of the main stem. Keep the soil moist around the transplanted shrub for the first few months, but do not overwater.

PROPAGATING SHRUBS BY LAYERING

1. Wounding the branch.
◆ In early spring, bend a healthy lower branch to touch the ground about 12 inches from the tip and dig a bowl-shaped hole about 6 inches deep there.
◆ Bend the branch into the hole. Where it touches the center of the hole, slit the branch diagonally about halfway through with a sharp knife and wedge a twig in the cut *(inset)*. Sprinkle the wound with rooting powder, a synthetic hormone available at garden centers.

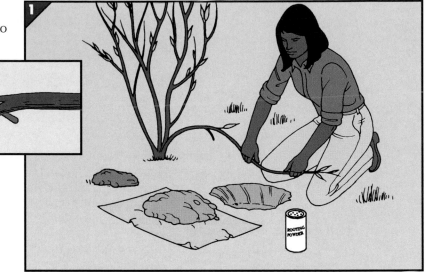

2. Anchoring the branch.
◆ Mix enough topsoil, peat moss, and sand, in equal parts, to fill the hole. then put about one fourth of the mixture into the hole.
◆ Bend the branch back into the hole with the cut facing down and cover it with soil mix. Anchor the branch with a pair of crossed sticks *(right),* and fill the hole with the remaining soil mix, making sure that 6 inches of the branch protrude above ground level.
◆ Water the soil mix thoroughly and set a rock over the crossed sticks to hold them in place.

3. Separating the new shrub.
◆ Do not disturb the branch until next spring, then dig it up. Pull away some soil to see if roots have developed at the cut. If three to five roots are present, sever the branch to free the new plant from the old one *(left);* if not, rebury the branch and check again in the fall.
◆ After detaching the branch, push gently on the rootball to slant the roots in the opposite direction from the tip. Plant the newly propagated shrub as you would any other, tilting the rootball so that the top of the plant points upward.

Like the houses they protect and adorn, trees need regular care, sometimes by professionals. You can perform the routine chores of low-level pruning, fertilizing, and pest control, but tasks such as bracing limbs with guy wires, or climbing to a high perch to cut them off, should be left to a specialist.

The Right Way to Prune: Judicious pruning can improve a tree's health. But because each cut wounds the tree, you can also do harm if you prune carelessly.

A tree walls off a wounded area with cells and chemical barriers that keep disease-causing organisms from invading healthy tissue. These guardians develop at the base of each branch in a swollen area called the branch collar.

Part of the collar is destroyed by pruning a branch flush to the trunk, a method favored in the past; the wound closes slowly, if at all. Cutting too far from the trunk is also a poor practice, since the stub is too far from the source of protective cells. To close properly, cuts must be made at a precise angle, just outside the collar *(opposite)*. Leave the wound untreated, or apply a thin coat of asphalt-based tree paint. Other paints retard closure.

Do your pruning in late winter or early spring, before the buds open.

Prune flowering trees just after the blooms fade, and remove any broken or diseased branches from all trees immediately.

Feeding Trees: To maintain normal growth, trees need a variety of nutrients, often provided in the form of fertilizer. Among the most effective fertilizers are organic materials such as cottonseed meal, bone meal, or blood meal.

Fertilizer works best when it is spread on the ground or injected as a liquid *(pages 74-75)*. You can also spray liquid fertilizer onto a tree's leaves *(page 76)*, or hammer fertilizer spikes around the drip line *(page 74)*. However, if the drip line is 30 inches or less from the trunk, do not use spikes.

The best time to apply fertilizer is in late autumn, when all the leaves have fallen and trees begin storing nutrients for the winter. You can also fertilize in early spring; for flowering trees, wait until they begin to bloom.

Whatever season you choose, avoid overuse of fertilizer. One or two applications a year is enough for young trees, and once every 3 to 5 years for mature ones.

Safe Pest Control: If a tree looks sickly or harbors bugs you do not recognize, call your local extension

service for a diagnosis. The prescription is likely to be a spray-on chemical, which must be handled with care. You can safely spray a tree up to 25 feet tall with the equipment shown on page 76. Hire a professional to treat larger trees.

Before you start, check local laws governing chemical spraying and study the instructions on the package label. Some pesticides must be mixed with water; dilute them exactly as directed. Wear protective clothing and keep children and pets out of the area.

If you prefer a nontoxic treatment, try dormant oil, a commercial mixture of mineral oil and water. Sprayed on a tree in early spring before leaves emerge, it coats and smothers aphids, scales, and mites, even before they hatch from eggs. Read the directions on the label carefully. Although harmless to humans, the oil can damage evergreens and certain species of beech, birch, and maple.

Another nontoxic approach is biological control, using a pest's natural enemies. A single ladybug, for example, can eat four dozen aphids a day, while a bacterium called Bt attacks gypsy-moth and other caterpillars but is harmless to other organisms. Ask your nursery operator or extension agent about pest fighters indigenous to your area.

 TOOLS

Pruning shears
Lopping shears
Pole shears
Pruning saw
Broadcast or trough spreader
Root-zone injector
Spray canister
Garden-hose sprayer

 **MATERIALS**

Dry fertilizer
Tree spikes
Fertilizer cartridges
Liquid fertilizer
Pesticide

 **SAFETY TIPS**

Wear gloves when handling fertilizers. Add goggles when cutting tree branches. Follow manufacturer's instructions precisely when spraying pesticides. Depending on toxicity, you may need to don not only gloves and goggles but boots, long sleeves, and a dust mask or cartridge respirator, as well.

THE ART OF PRUNING

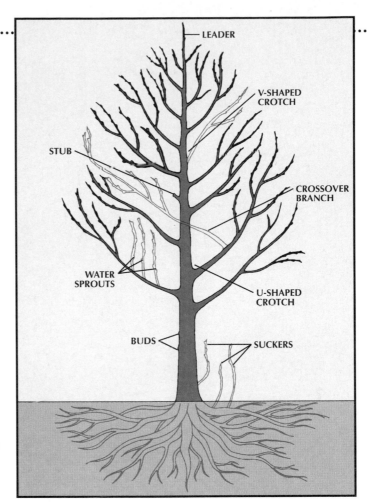

The basic guidelines.

Well-formed young trees have a straight central branch, or leader, extending from the top; the main limbs have U-shaped crotches evenly distributed around the trunk at least a foot apart vertically. To maintain this strong, balanced framework, prune away any undesirable features:

◆ Remove branches having a tight, V-shaped crotch, which makes a weak joint.

◆ Cut off suckers or water sprouts—which can grow anywhere on a tree and have no lateral branches—as well as any buds from which new suckers and water sprouts might grow.

◆ Dispose of branch stubs, dead or broken limbs, and small branches that grow toward the trunk or across larger limbs; crossover growth can damage the trunk and other branches by rubbing against them.

◆ Periodically thin inner branches of mature trees to admit light. On deciduous trees, remove low limbs that keep you from walking under the tree. Leave the lower limbs on evergreens in place.

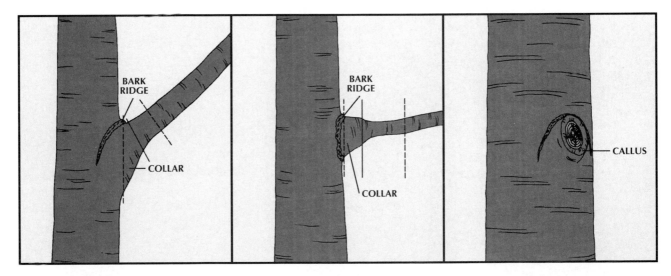

Proper pruning cuts.

Two features of a branch govern the position and angle of a pruning cut—the thick collar at the base of the branch and the dark ridge in the bark of the parent branch or trunk.

On mature deciduous trees, trim branches off square near the collar *(solid line, above left)*. Do not cut into the collar or the ridge, and do not leave a stub *(dotted lines)*. A branch on a very young deciduous tree or an evergreen may have a large collar and a bark ridge that encircles the base *(above, center)*. Prune just outside the collar and parallel to the bark ridge *(solid line)*, neither leaving a stub nor cutting into the ridge or the collar *(dotted lines)*.

In a year or so, a hard callus should form at the edge of the wound *(above, right)*, later closing over the cut.

THREE TOOLS FOR SMALL BRANCHES

Shearing small sprouts.
Use pruning shears to sever buds and small branches that are up to $\frac{1}{4}$ inch thick. Cut as close to the trunk as you can without damaging the bark.

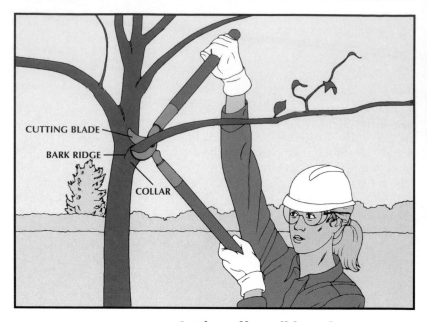

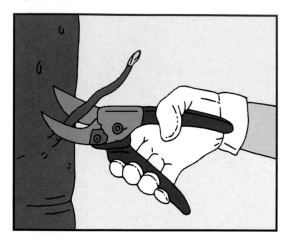

Cutting off small branches.
To remove a branch up to 1 inch thick, set the cutting blade of a pair of lopping shears on top of the limb, with the side of the blade against the trunk or supporting branch. Angle the lower blade away from the bark ridge and the collar, and bring the handles of the shears together in a single smooth motion. Do not twist the shears or use them to tear the branch from the tree. If the shears do not make a clean cut on the first attempt, sharpen them *(page 8)* or switch to a saw.

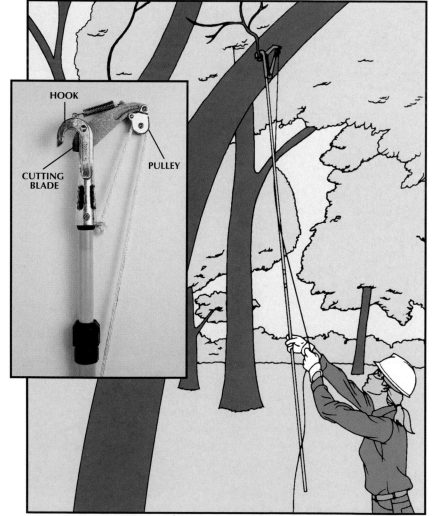

Extendable shears.
Pole shears can cut branches as big as 1 inch in diameter and reach branches up to 15 feet overhead. The pole consists of a telescoping plastic or wooden shaft. A cutting blade under a stationary hook is operated by a cord that runs through a pulley to increase leverage *(photograph)*.

◆ Place the hook over the base of the branch in the position shown on page 71. Wrap the cord once around the pole to keep the shaft from bowing, and pull the cord sharply. Cut close enough to the branch collar so no stub remains.
◆ If the severed branch hangs in the tree, pull it down with the head of the shears, taking care not to break other branches.

SAWING OFF A LIMB

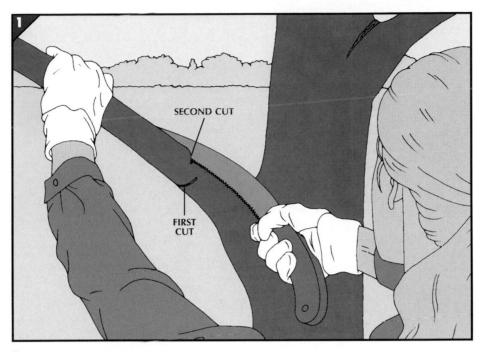

1. Removing the branch.

◆ When cutting a branch that is up to 3 inches thick, first trim off any secondary limbs. This will serve to lighten the branch and keep it from catching in the tree as it falls.

◆ Use a pruning saw to cut halfway through the bottom of the branch, about a foot from the trunk; this cut will stop bark from tearing loose when the branch falls.

◆ About an inch outside the first cut, saw through the branch from the top. When this second cut is halfway through the branch, the limb will snap off, leaving a stub.

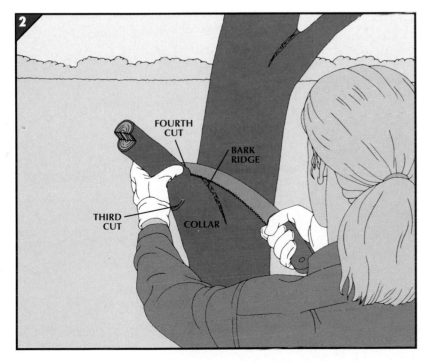

2. Trimming the stub.

◆ For the third cut, saw 1 inch into the underside of the stub, just outside the branch collar and at a right angle to the stub.

◆ Make the fourth cut at the crotch of the stub, just outside the bark ridge at the base of the stub *(left)*. Support the stub with one hand and saw downward to meet the third cut.

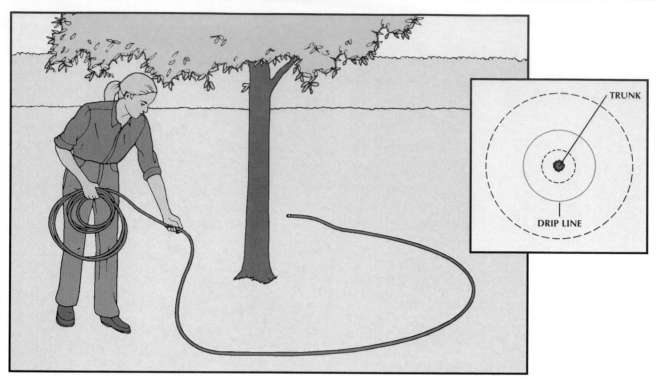

Mapping for surface fertilizer.

◆ Lay a string or garden hose around the tree at the drip line, which is directly below the tree's outermost leaves.
◆ Mark a second circle about two-thirds of the way in from the drip line to the center, but not less than 5 feet from the trunk. Mark a third circle about twice the drip-line distance from the trunk *(inset)*.
◆ Using a broadcast or trough spreader, spread tree fertilizer over the area between the inner- and outermost circles.

Placing tree spikes.

◆ Mark the drip line of your tree as for surface fertilizer, above.
◆ For each inch of trunk diameter, drive a spike into the ground along the drip line. Space the spikes evenly, and while hammering, shield the tops with the protective plastic cap provided.

INJECTING FERTILIZER BY WATER PRESSURE

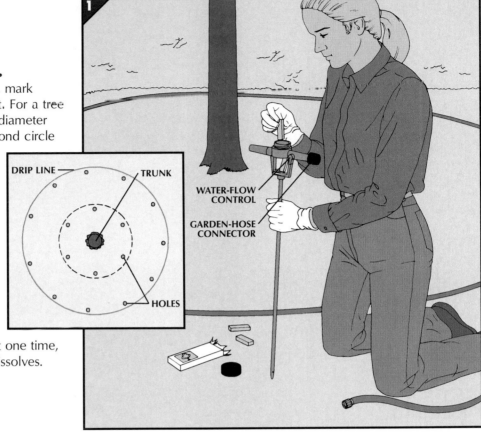

1. Preparing a root-zone injector.

◆ Along the tree's drip line *(opposite),* mark spots for an injection every 2 to 3 feet. For a tree having a trunk more than 4 inches in diameter and widespread branches, mark a second circle halfway to the trunk and plot injector locations along it *(inset).*

◆ Consult the fertilizer box for the number of fertilizer cartridges needed for each inch of tree trunk diameter. Divide the total by the number of injection points to get the number of cartridges per injection.

◆ Load the root-zone injector for one injection by unscrewing the reservoir cap and dropping in water-soluble fertilizer cartridges. If the reservoir is too small for all of them at one time, replenish the supply as the fertilizer dissolves.

DRIP LINE · TRUNK · HOLES

WATER-FLOW CONTROL

GARDEN-HOSE CONNECTOR

2. Using the injector.

◆ Close the water-flow control valve and connect a garden hose to the injector.

◆ Turn the water on to a medium flow, and open the control valve on the injector just enough to permit water to trickle out of the tube.

◆ Slowly push the tube into the soil, twisting it back and forth until it reaches a depth of 6 to 8 inches. In hard ground, allow the water to soften the dirt and ease the way.

◆ For trees with shallow roots, set the control valve halfway between OFF and HALF ON; for more deeply rooted trees, set it to HALF ON; for very large, well-established trees, start at HALF ON, then turn the valve to ON after the first minute. Leave the injector in place until the fertilizer has dissolved, then turn the water off, pull out the tube, and move to the next injection spot.

A HAND-PUMPED SPRAYER FOR SMALL JOBS

A pressurized canister.

◆ To fill the canister, remove the pump assembly. Pour liquid fertilizer or pesticide into a small amount of water in the canister, then add the rest of the water needed to dilute the chemical. Mix powdered chemicals thoroughly with the full measure of water in a bucket before pouring it into the canister.

◆ Screw in the pump, and vigorously raise and lower the handle several times to pressurize the tank. Aim the nozzle upward and squeeze the pistol grip to saturate the undersides of leaves. Adjust the fineness of the spray, if necessary, by turning the nozzle tip, and repressurize the tank whenever the spray weakens.

PISTOL GRIP

PRESSURE-PUMP HANDLE

USING A GARDEN-HOSE SPRAYER

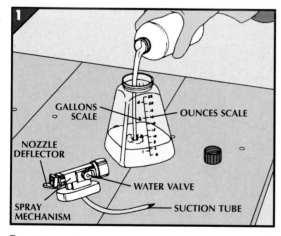

GALLONS SCALE · OUNCES SCALE

NOZZLE DEFLECTOR

WATER VALVE

SPRAY MECHANISM · SUCTION TUBE

1. Filling the sprayer.

◆ Pour concentrated liquid fertilizer or pesticide into the reservoir, using the ounces scale on its side to measure the desired amount.

◆ Add water slowly while watching the gallons scale, stopping when the mixture reaches the level that matches the amount of spray solution you need.

◆ Screw on the spray mechanism, close the water valve, and gently shake the sprayer.

2. Using the sprayer.

Connect the sprayer to a garden hose and open the spigot. With the sprayer pointed at the tree, open the water valve; when spraying dormant oil, saturate both the trunk and the limbs. To control the force of the spray, turn the garden-hose spigot. Direct the spray upward with the nozzle deflector. Doing so allows you to keep the sprayer level enough for the suction tube to siphon chemicals into the spray.

How to Move a Tree

A tree's size, weight, and stability make it seem a permanent part of the landscape, but there are times when it is necessary to move a tree. Small or young trees, for example, may need to be temporarily stored out of the way of construction projects. And some trees should be permanently moved away from areas with poor drainage, unfavorable soil conditions, or extreme wind. Mature trees in good health can also be relocated to fit a new landscape plan.

A Matter of Size: In general, those trees up to 10 feet tall with trunks up to 3 inches thick can be moved with relative ease and can be expected to thrive after the experience. Larger trees, however, are unwieldy and are more vulnerable to shock; the job of moving them should be evaluated—and usually performed—by a professional.

Planning Ahead: The best time to move a deciduous tree is late autumn or early spring, when the tree is dormant. An evergreen can be moved at any time. Several months to a year in advance, cut about half of the horizontal roots, but not the vertical taproot. Make these cuts in three 60-degree arcs 24 to 30 inches from the trunk *(Step 1, below)*.

Pruning the tree *(pages 70-73)* in advance lessens the danger of shock by allowing new feeder roots time to form before the tree is moved. To compensate for the lost root capacity, however, prune away about a third of the branches.

 TOOLS

Spade
Shovel
Rake

 MATERIALS

Burlap
Twine
Mulch

 SAFETY TIPS

Wear work gloves when digging and a back brace to reduce the chance of injury when moving heavy objects such as trees.

1. Pruning the roots.

Using a spade with a well-sharpened blade, sever the roots in a circle 24 to 30 inches wide around the trunk, re-cutting roots where they were pruned in advance. Push the blade into the ground at about a 30-degree angle toward the trunk *(dotted line),* so that the rootball will taper.

EARLIER PRUNING

2. Uprooting the tree.

◆ Excavate an access trench, 18 inches deep, around the rootball.

◆ Thrust the blade of a spade—the long-handled variety works best—under the tree to sever the taproot and any other uncut roots *(above)*.

◆ With a helper, lift the tree by the rootball and place it on a square of burlap. Removing a tree with low branches may be easier if you work the burlap under the rootball before lifting the tree from the hole *(page 66)*.

3. Bagging the rootball.

◆ Draw the burlap up around the ball on all sides, twisting the excess around the trunk.

◆ Run twine around the ball in several directions, tilting the tree to get the string under it.

◆ When you have bound the rootball into a neat package, wrap the twine around the trunk several times and tie it off.

4. Storing the tree.

If you can replant the tree within a week, set it in a shady spot, cover the rootball with mulch, and water it.

To store a tree for longer periods, dig a hole about half the rootball depth in a shady area, protected from wind. Tip the rootball into the hole and cover it with a 6-inch layer of mulch *(left)*. Keep the rootball moist.

Trees are available for planting in three forms: balled and burlapped, container grown, or bare rooted. Before buying any young tree, however, use the charts on pages 116 to 119 to find out which species thrive in your area. Prepare a soil mixture for the planting hole as you would for a shrub *(page 67)*.

Planting a Tree: Bare-rooted trees, usually sold by mail-order nurseries, are generally smaller, younger, and less expensive than the others. Start such trees in the early spring, within a day or two of their arrival. The technique for setting a bare-rooted tree into the ground appears on the next page.

You can plant container-grown and balled and burlapped trees at any time of the year. A balled and burlapped tree is planted exactly as a similarly packaged shrub *(pages 67-68)*—as is a container-grown tree, once you have slipped the plastic pot from around the rootball as described below.

Care after Planting: Unless the tree has been container grown or pruned at the nursery, cut away about one-third of the branches *(pages 70-73)*. Wrap a plastic tree protector around the base of the trunk to prevent damage to the lower bark *(page 80)*.

Brace or guy trees in areas where high winds or playing children may loosen their roots *(page 81)*. Never tie braces or guy wires taut; root systems strengthen faster when a tree can sway gently in the wind. Guying kits are available at garden centers. You can assemble a tree brace yourself using galvanized wire and pieces of old garden hose.

Finally, water a newly planted tree well; it needs the equivalent of an inch of rainfall a week during the growing season.

TOOLS

Utility knife
Pruning shears
Spade
4-pound maul

MATERIALS

Tree protector
2-by-2 stakes
Cloth strips
Old garden hose
Galvanized wire

CONTAINER-GROWN SPECIMENS

Trees from plastic pots.

◆ Slide the pot off the rootball, tapping or flexing the sides of the pot as necessary to loosen it.
◆ If the tree you buy has circling roots *(right)*, gently unwind them. Cut off large curling and matted roots with pruning shears.
◆ With a utility knife or sharp kitchen knife, score the rootball 1 inch deep from top to bottom in four or five locations that are evenly spaced *(inset)*.
◆ Plant the tree as shown for shrubs on pages 67-68.

TREES WITH BARE ROOTS

SOIL-LEVEL MARK

1. Positioning the roots.
◆ Dig a planting hole *(page 67)* about one and a half times as deep as the length of the tree's longest root; make the hole about as wide as it is deep.
◆ Pile soil in the center of the hole, then gently spread the tree roots over the mound. With a straight board as a guide *(above)*, adjust the mound so the soil-level mark on the tree trunk falls no lower than ground level.

2. Filling in around the roots.
◆ Holding the tree vertically, scoop soil into the hole. Pack the soil gently but firmly around the roots to eliminate air pockets.
◆ Fill the hole two-thirds with soil, one-third with water. After the water has seeped away, add soil to ground level. Build a soil basin as shown in Step 5 on page 68, fill it with water, then mulch.

CARING FOR RECENT TRANSPLANTS

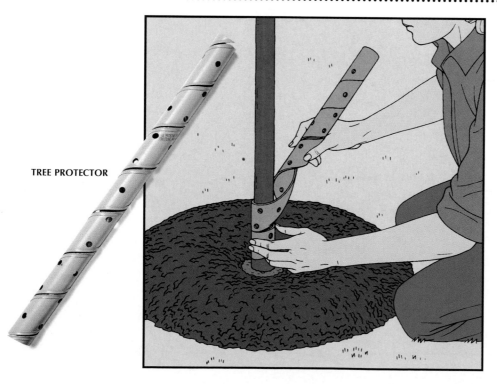

TREE PROTECTOR

Protecting tender bark.
◆ Push back the soil at the tree trunk's base to a depth of about 2 inches.
◆ Coil a plastic tree protector around the trunk *(left)*. After installing the protector, slide it to the base of the tree. Replace the loosened soil.
◆ Tree protectors are designed to expand as the plant grows. At least once a year, check the protector for binding and loosen it as needed. Remove the protector after 2 to 3 years.

Bracing small trees.

◆ For a trunk less than 3 inches thick, position a pair of 6-foot, 2-by-2 stakes next to the planting hole. With a 4-pound maul, drive them at least 18 inches into the ground.

◆ Tie one end of a cloth strip near the top of one post. Loop the cloth once around the trunk, leaving about 1 inch of slack. Tie the other end of the cloth to the second post, again leaving an inch of slack.

◆ Remove the bracing when the tree is firmly rooted—no later than a year after planting.

Guying a tree.

◆ For trunks 3 inches or more in diameter, drive three notched stakes into the ground outside the planting hole.

◆ Thread the end of a guy wire through a 1-foot-long length of garden hose. Loop the hose around the trunk above a branch, then twist the wire around itself to secure the hose to the tree. Tie the other end of the wire to the notch in a stake.

◆ Add two more guy wires, then adjust all three of them to allow the tree to sway slightly.

4 The Finishing Touches

A carpet of green, punctuated by trees and shrubs, supplies almost everything needed for a well-landscaped yard. Yet a constructed element or two in the plan can make for an appealing finale. An addition as simple as a new flower bed or as ambitious as a garden pool can showcase favorite varieties or establish a fresh vantage point from which to appreciate the fruits of your landscaping labors.

A rock garden in bloom →

Clearly defined areas set aside for flowers or shrubs are part of any landscaping plan. Beds for such plantings can be dug into the ground or boldly raised above the surrounding terrain.

The Simple Approach: Locate ground-level beds in an area of your yard with good drainage. Apart from properly prepared soil, the only requirement for the bed is a barrier of edging to keep out grass and weeds.

Plastic edging comes in 20-foot rolls and includes a coupler for joining sections. Purchase plastic stakes separately to anchor the edging to the ground.

Aluminum edging in a choice of colors is sold in 16-foot lengths. It is molded with flanges and grooves for joining sections and comes with one anchor stake for each 4 feet of edging.

Both metal and plastic edgings bend easily, making them especially suitable for irregularly shaped beds. Right-angle couplers are also available for installing both kinds of edging around a bed with corners that are square. However, rectangular beds are also ideally suited to the mortarless brick edging shown on page 86. Whatever edging you choose for a rectangular bed, use the triangulation method *(below)* to lay out square corners.

Raised Beds: In locations with poor drainage or crossed by large tree roots, a ground-level bed is impractical. The solution is an aboveground bed of soil framed by walls between 12 inches and 24 inches high.

Among the materials suitable for building a raised bed are stone and brick, but pressure-treated timbers are by far the easiest to work with *(pages 86-87)*. After you have assembled the walls, fill the frame of the bed with amended soil and compost *(pages 28-31)*.

TOOLS

Garden spade	Carpenter's level
Mattock	Maul
Edging tool	Electric drill
Circular saw	$\frac{1}{4}$-inch and $\frac{3}{8}$-inch
Sawhorses	auger bits

MATERIALS

Garden hose	Mason's cord
Stakes and string	$\frac{3}{8}$- by 24-inch
Edging	reinforcing rods
Chalk	10-inch galvanized
6-by-6 pressure-	spikes
treated timbers	

SAFETY TIPS

Gloves protect your hands during spadework. Wear a back brace to reduce the risk of injury when digging.

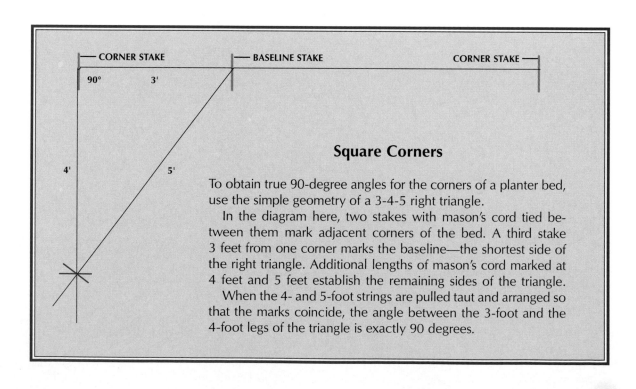

CORNER STAKE   BASELINE STAKE   CORNER STAKE

90°   3'

4'   5'

Square Corners

To obtain true 90-degree angles for the corners of a planter bed, use the simple geometry of a 3-4-5 right triangle.

In the diagram here, two stakes with mason's cord tied between them mark adjacent corners of the bed. A third stake 3 feet from one corner marks the baseline—the shortest side of the right triangle. Additional lengths of mason's cord marked at 4 feet and 5 feet establish the remaining sides of the triangle.

When the 4- and 5-foot strings are pulled taut and arranged so that the marks coincide, the angle between the 3-foot and the 4-foot legs of the triangle is exactly 90 degrees.

MAKING A GROUND-LEVEL BED

HOSE

BED AREA

1. Outlining the bed.
◆ For a curved bed, lay out a garden hose in the desired shape; for a bed with straight sides, use stakes and string.
◆ Stand outside the bed and place the blade of a garden spade against the inside edge of the hose or string. Holding the shaft at a slight angle, push the blade 4 to 6 inches deep *(left)*.
◆ Cut along the outline of the bed in the same manner to make a continuous slit in the turf.

2. Preparing the bed.
◆ Working inside the bed, make a second cut 6 inches inside the first, angling the spade to re-move wedges of sod from between the two cuts.
◆ Strip off the sod in the remainder of the bed with a spade or mattock *(left)*. Compost the sod, or set it aside for transplanting to another part of the yard.
◆ Prepare the soil for planting as described on pages 28-31.
◆ Using a spade or edging tool, form the edge of the bed into a V-shaped trench about 4 inches deep *(inset)*.

EDGING CHOICES

Plastic.

◆ Unroll the edging and lay it flat for an hour.

◆ Meanwhile, deepen the trench with a garden trowel to leave only the hose-shaped rim of the edging exposed.

◆ Bend the edging to match the trench contours and set it in place. To link edging sections, insert a plastic coupler halfway into the upper rim of one section, then slide the next section onto the coupler *(right)*.

◆ To anchor the edging, drive plastic stakes through the barb molded into the bottom. Place the point of the stake at the barb and, to assure a 45-degree angle, hold the beveled tip against the edging *(photograph)*. Position stakes at the ends of the edging, the joints, and at 4-foot intervals between them.

◆ Backfill the trench and tamp on both sides of the edging until only the rim can be seen.

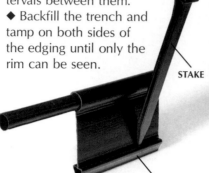

STAKE

BARB

RIM

COUPLER

Aluminum.

◆ Deepen the trench to leave $\frac{1}{2}$ inch of the edging above ground level.

◆ Stand the edging alongside the bed and gently bend it to match the curves of the trench.

◆ To join lengths of edging, align the flanges at the top and bottom of one section with matching grooves in the other *(photograph)*. Push the pieces together, overlapping them at least 2 inches.

◆ To shorten the edging, increase the overlap at joints or disassemble sections for trimming with a hacksaw.

◆ Set the edging in the trench, and secure it at 4-foot intervals. To do so, hook the 12-inch aluminum stakes over the top of the edging and pound them into the ground.

◆ Backfill and tamp on both sides of the edging.

FLANGE

GROOVE

Brick.

◆ Widen the bottom of the trench with a mattock blade to a depth of about 5 inches. Tamp the trench bottom with the end of a 2-by-4.

◆ About 3 inches above the center of the trench, stretch a string between two stakes.

◆ Set a brick in one corner of the trench to prop a row of bricks set at an angle in the trench along one side of the bed. Place the bricks so that their top edges touch the string *(right)*.

◆ Brick the bed's other sides in the same fashion.

CONSTRUCTING A RAISED BED

1. Measuring and cutting timbers.

◆ Lay timbers to be cut across a pair of sturdy sawhorses. Mark each timber one timber-width ($5\frac{1}{2}$ inches for a 6-by-6) shorter than the exterior dimensions of the bed you plan to build. If the sides of the bed are more than one timber in length, plan your cutting to stagger joints from course to course.

◆ Fully extend the blade of a circular saw. Make one pass through the timber, then turn it over and make a second pass to complete the cut *(right)*.

2. Anchoring the base.

◆ Dig a trench 2 inches deep with a mattock or spade and lay the bottom course of timbers in the trench.

◆ With a carpenter's level, check that the timbers are level, adjusting the depth of the trench as needed to make them so.

◆ Drill $\frac{3}{8}$-inch pilot holes for reinforcing rods, 6 to 8 inches from both ends of all four timbers.

◆ With a maul, drive a 24-inch length of $\frac{3}{8}$-inch reinforcing rod through each hole and into the ground, marking rod locations on the fronts of the timbers in chalk.

CHALK MARK

3. Adding the upper courses.

◆ Lay the remaining timber courses, constructing corners as shown at right.

◆ For each course, drill a $\frac{1}{4}$-inch pilot hole, 6 inches deep, at all four corners, about 1 inch from timber center-lines. In addition, drill a hole midway along every timber and 6 to 8 inches from the end that is not in the corner. Make sure that no hole coincides with a chalk mark on the course below.

◆ Drive 10-inch galvanized spikes into the holes, then mark the spike positions with chalk on the front of all but the top course.

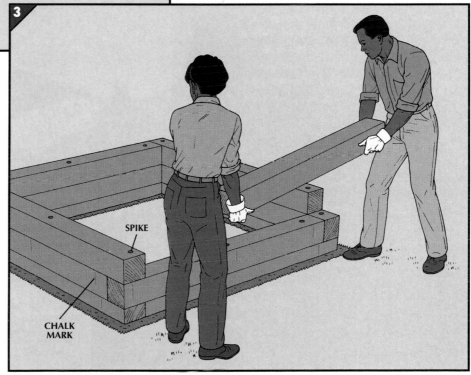

SPIKE

CHALK MARK

Decorative Wooden Containers for Plants

Wooden containers, as landscape elements, not only sustain small parcels of greenery on a deck or on a patio, but they are visually appealing in their own right. The easy-to-build flower box that is shown below requires only two board sizes for the frame and two sizes for the trim. You can readily adapt the instructions on this and the following pages to make a container of any length you wish. The modular design of the freestanding planter with optional benches that is shown on pages 91 to 93 allows you to use your imagination to fill a space of just about any size or shape.

Treating the Wood: Because the chemicals in pressure-treated wood can harm many plants, buy ordinary lumber for planters and flower boxes. Countersink the heads of all finishing nails and plug the holes with waterproof wood putty, then paint or stain the wood to seal it. Before filling a container with soil for planting, cover the bottom with galvanized screening and 1 to 2 inches of gravel.

 TOOLS

Combination square	Electric drill with
Circular saw	$\frac{1}{16}$-, $\frac{1}{8}$-, and $\frac{3}{4}$-
Hammer	inch bits
Plane	Caulk gun
Clamps	Backsaw and miter
Saber saw	box

 MATERIALS FOR FLOWER BOX

1-by-6	Caulk
1-by-8	1$\frac{1}{4}$- and 2-inch galvanized
1-by-2	finishing nails
1-by-3	Waterproof wood putty

 MATERIALS FOR PLANTER

2-by-4s	2$\frac{1}{2}$-inch galvanized
2-by-2s	wood screws
2$\frac{1}{2}$-inch galvanized	$\frac{3}{8}$-inch plywood for
common nails	spacers
2$\frac{1}{2}$-inch galvanized	
finishing nails	

Anatomy of a flower box.
This attractive flower box has angled sides that not only add to its appeal but help prevent the weight of plants and damp soil from pushing out the bottom, which has holes bored through it to promote drainage. Trim around the top serves as a handle for lifting the box. Stands raise the box from the surface of a deck or patio, or allow it to be set atop a 2-by-6 deck railing.

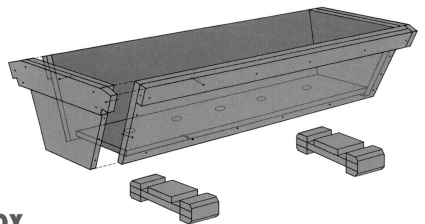

BUILDING A FLOWER BOX

1. Cutting out the pieces.
◆ To mark the end pieces, draw a baseline with a combination square 1 inch from the end of a 1-by-8. Along one edge, mark the board 9 inches and 13$\frac{1}{2}$ inches from the line.
◆ On the opposite edge, mark the board 2$\frac{1}{4}$ inches, 6$\frac{3}{4}$ inches, and 15$\frac{3}{4}$ inches from the line.
◆ Join the marks on each side with three straight lines as shown at right, and saw along the center of the lines.
◆ Place one end piece on top of the other and sand the edges as necessary to make the ends identical.
◆ Cut the two side pieces to the desired length from a 1-by-8.
◆ From a 1-by-6, cut the bottom 1$\frac{1}{2}$ inches shorter than the sides.

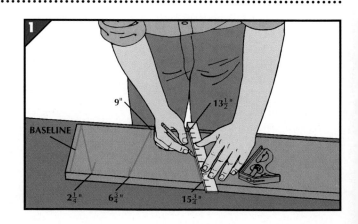

2. Attaching the sides to the ends.

◆ With a $\frac{1}{16}$-inch bit, drill four evenly spaced pilot holes along a line $\frac{3}{8}$ inch from each end of each side piece. Place a 2-inch galvanized finishing nail in each hole.

◆ Spread glue sparingly on one edge of an end piece. Place the end piece top down on the floor with one corner against a wall for support. Mate a side piece to the end piece, and drive the four nails as shown at right.

◆ Repeat the process for the remaining three joints between the end pieces and the sides.

3. Shaping the bottom.

With a plane, bevel the edges of the bottom to fit between the sides:

◆ First, draw lines the length of the board $\frac{1}{4}$ inch in from each side edge, and then draw diagonal lines across the ends of the board as shown in the inset.

◆ Clamp the bottom to a work surface with the marked side up, protecting the board with scraps of wood.

◆ Plane both edges to the pencil lines, then check the fit of the bottom against the sides of the box. Plane or sand the bottom as needed to match the bevel to the slant of the sides.

◆ With the bottom out of the box, drill $\frac{3}{4}$-inch drainage holes along the center of the board, 3 inches from each end and about 7 inches apart.

4. Attaching the bottom.

◆ Put the bottom in the box, then measure the distance between the top of the box and the bottom *(near right)*.

◆ Add $\frac{3}{8}$ inch to this measurement and mark both sides of the box at both ends *(far right)*. Remove the bottom and connect the marks with straight lines.

◆ Along the lines, drill $\frac{1}{16}$-inch pilot holes through the sides, 6 inches apart.

◆ Spread glue sparingly along the beveled edges of the bottom, place it in the box, and drive 2-inch galvanized finishing nails through the pilot holes and into the bottom.

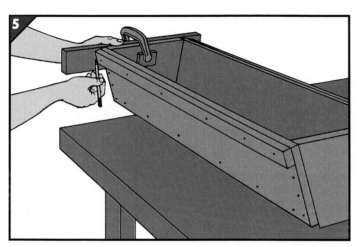

5. Trimming the top.

◆ Cut two pieces of 1-by-2 the length of the sides; drill $\frac{1}{16}$-inch pilot holes through them, 6 inches apart.

◆ Glue and nail the side trim flush with the tops and ends of the sides with $1\frac{1}{4}$-inch galvanized finishing nails. Sand the trim flush with the ends of the box.

◆ For the end trim, clamp a piece of 1-by-3 to the box *(left)*, and trace the shape of the box on the back of the 1-by-3. Unclamp it and cut along the lines with a saber saw. Make a similar piece for the other end.

◆ Drill $\frac{1}{16}$-inch pilot holes in each end trim piece as shown in the anatomy drawing on page 88, then glue and nail the trim to the ends of the box.

◆ Sand the trim to smooth and make the edges flush with the box's contours.

6. Building the stands.

Two stands are sufficient for boxes less than three feet long; build a third stand for longer versions.

◆ For each stand, cut pieces $4\frac{1}{2}$ inches long and 9 inches long from a piece of 1-by-4.

◆ Cut a 15-inch length of 1-by-2 and lightly bevel one edge with a plane. Then cut four $3\frac{1}{2}$-inch pieces from the 1-by-2.

◆ To test the fit, assemble the stands on the floor as shown at right and set the box on them. Sand the ends of the shorter 1-by-4s if necessary to make the box sit firmly.

◆ Glue and nail all the pieces to the longer 1-by-4s.

1 x 2

BEVELED
EDGES

$4\frac{1}{2}$" 1 x 4

9" 1 x 4

PLANTERS WITH BENCHES

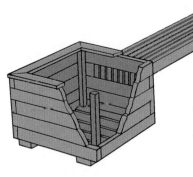

A modular system.

Boxes for planting can be freestanding units or components of a larger assemblage having one or more benches. A box consists of five courses of 2-by-4s with a 2-by-2 brace in each corner and a cap of mitered 2-by-4s. These dimensions yield a planter sufficiently large for an ornamental shrub or an interesting flower arrangement, yet not too heavy to be placed on a deck. Each bench uses seven 2-by-4s, up to 8 feet long. Because the presence of benches affects box construction, plan the unit before you begin building it.

1. Building the base.

◆ Cut four 2-foot lengths of 2-by-4 and set them on edge to form a square. For best results, orient the end grain of the pieces as shown in the photo at right.

◆ With a $\frac{1}{8}$-inch bit, drill two pilot holes through the face of each 2-by-4 where it overlaps the adjacent piece, then fasten each corner with $2\frac{1}{2}$-inch galvanized nails.

◆ For the feet, cut two 2-by-4s, $25\frac{3}{4}$ inches long. Drill two pilot holes at each end of the feet, then lay them across the frame, about 2 inches in from the edges. Square the frame and nail the feet in place.

◆ Cut five pieces of 2-by-4, $22\frac{1}{4}$ inches long. Turn the structure over and nail the 2-by-4s to the feet as shown above, leaving uniform drainage spaces between the boards.

A Jig for Cutting 2-by-4s

For a planter that looks professionally built, it is essential that all the 2-by-4 pieces be exactly the same length. If you don't have a table saw, you can achieve the results with a circular saw and the jig shown below.

A 2-by-6 at least 6 feet long serves as the base. Near one end, screw a piece of 2-by-2 to act as an end stop. A little more than 2 feet from the end stop, screw an 18-inch 2-by-2 to the base, flush against the edge, as a side stop. Mark a 2-by-4 with a cut line 2 feet from one end, and set the board against the side and end stops. Place the blade of your saw at the cut line, then set a piece of $\frac{3}{4}$-inch plywood alongside the saw's baseplate. Put the saw aside and screw the plywood to the side stop as a saw guide.

To use the jig, set your saw for a 2-inch depth. Slide a 2-by-4 against the stops, place the saw baseplate against the guide, and cut through.

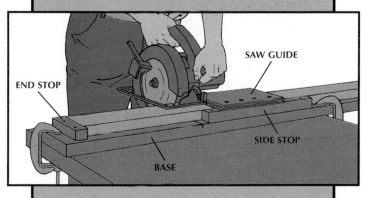

END STOP

SAW GUIDE

SIDE STOP

BASE

2. Putting the box together.

◆ For the corner braces, cut four 16-inch lengths of 2-by-2.

◆ Hold a brace firmly in one corner of the base and drill $\frac{1}{8}$-inch pilot holes through the 2-by-2 and into the 2-by-4s at the corner, offsetting the holes so they do not meet. Attach the brace with $2\frac{1}{2}$-inch galvanized screws. Repeat at the other corners.

◆ Assemble the second course as you did the frame for the base, and slip it over the braces, forming the corner-joint pattern shown at left. Drill pilot holes and screw the corner braces to this course.

3. Finishing the box.

For boxes without benches, repeat the preceding step to add the remaining three courses. However, if your plan includes benches, stop after the third course and build the fourth course as shown here—three-sided to support one bench end or two-sided to support the ends of two benches.

◆ Nail a two- or three-sided course together, as called for. Lay it on the third course, and screw the cor- ner braces to it. Set the fifth course in place, supporting it with a scrap piece of 2-by-4 in the case of a two-sided fourth course (inset). Screw the corner braces to the fifth course.

◆ For the cap, cut four lengths of 2-by-4, $26\frac{1}{2}$ inches long, then miter the ends with a backsaw and a miter box. Nail the cap pieces to the fifth course with finishing nails, set the heads, and hide the holes with water-proof wood putty.

SPACER

1. Fitting bench slats.

◆ Place the boxes in their final locations with open sides of the fourth course facing each other.

◆ Measure the distance between the interior faces of the boxes, and cut seven 2-by-4 slats to that length.

◆ Insert the slats on edge into the space in the fourth course so that the ends are flush with the interior faces of the boxes (above).

◆ Place $\frac{3}{8}$-inch spacers—plywood works well—between the slats at both ends of the bench (inset), then center the bench in the fourth course.

2. Completing the fourth course.

◆ Measure the gap between the bench and the inside edge of the fourth course (left), and cut a 2-by-4 filler to match. Fit the filler into the gap, then nail through the fourth course into the end of the filler to secure it. (You need not anchor the filler to the bench.)

◆ On the other side of the bench, slide a piece of 2-by-4 into the gap and against the bench. Mark a trim line on the board using the outside of the box as a guide, then cut the filler and nail it in place.

Support for Climbing Plants

Flowering or fruit-bearing plants gracefully climbing a wooden framework bring a three-dimensional touch to your landscape design. Along an exterior wall, a trellis can give plants maximum exposure to the sun, shield them from extreme weather, or provide privacy for a pool or a patio. Freestanding post-and-beam arbors control and support heavy, spreading vines like grapes and wisteria and at the same time add a touch of classic design.

The Proper Location: Mount lightweight wood or plastic trellises at least 2 inches from the house with wooden spacers. The gap lets air circulate and helps prevent vines from attaching themselves to the wall. Erect sturdier trellises intended for bushy plants at least 6 inches from the wall.

If you want an arbor that is big enough to walk under, build it at least 4 feet wide and 7 feet high, with beams and rafters overhanging the corner posts at least 1 foot on all sides. Choose a site for the arbor that is level and use the squaring method described on page 84 to locate the corner posts.

Build to Last: Trellises and arbors must be strong enough to support mature plants in full bloom and to withstand the worst weather your region offers.

Rot-resistant redwood or cedar are excellent choices for trellises and arbors. Neither requires painting or sealing as ordinary pine does. And unlike pressure-treated lumber, they contain no preservatives harmful to some plants. No matter what material you choose, assemble the structure with corrosion-resistant galvanized nails and other hardware.

TOOLS

Screwdriver
Carpenter's level
Hammer
Saw
Spade or post-hole digger
Adjustable wrench
Stepladders

MATERIALS

4-by-4 posts
2-by-4s
1-by-2s, -6s, and -8s
$\frac{1}{4}$-by-2 lath
Hooks and eyes
Strap hinges
6-inch carriage bolts, washers, and nuts
Galvanized nails
Galvanized rafter ties

TWO VARIETIES OF TRELLIS

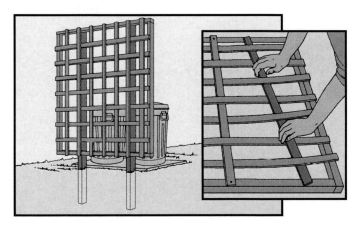

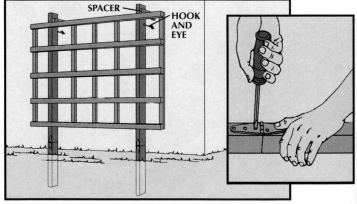

Choosing a trellis.
A simple trellis starts with a pair of 2-by-4 uprights, located parallel to a wall or at right angles to it and set at least 2 feet into the ground.

A trellis to support light vines *(above, left)* begins as a rectangular frame of 2-by-4s nailed to the posts, flush with the tops. The frame should be 1 foot shorter than the height of the posts and at least 2 feet wider than the distance between them. You can weave $\frac{1}{4}$- by 2-inch lath into a uniform grid *(inset)* or buy basket weave lattice and cut it to fit the frame.

For heavier vines, a grid of 1-by-2s (with the posts serving as two of the verticals) provides sturdy support *(above, right).* Spacers that are made of 1-by-2s and sets of hooks and eyes hold the trellis 6 inches from the wall. You can cut and hinge the posts *(inset)* about 6 inches from the ground to permit tipping the trellis outward for pruning the vines or painting the house.

A POST-AND-BEAM ARBOR

1. Setting the posts.

◆ For each 4-by-4 corner post, dig a hole 3 feet deep with a spade or posthole digger. In soft or sandy soil, place a flat stone or brick at the bottom of each hole.

◆ Stand a post in the center of a hole with the sides aligned to the rectangular layout. While a helper uses a level to hold the post vertical *(left)*, tamp soil around the post with a 2-by-4 in successive layers a few inches deep until the hole is filled.

◆ To keep the post plumb, temporarily nail two braces to the post and to stakes in the ground.

◆ When the first post is in place, stand the other posts alongside it one at a time and mark them at the height of the first. Turn the posts over, then set and brace them in the remaining holes to the depth marked.

2. Mounting the beams.

◆ Measure and cut four 1-by-8s for the beams. With a helper, lift a board even with the top of one pair of posts, the ends extending equally. Fasten the board to one post with a nail, then level the board and nail it to the other post. Mount a second on the posts' opposite sides.

◆ Drill two $\frac{1}{2}$-inch holes through the boards and post, 1 inch from post and board edges *(inset)*. Insert 6-inch carriage bolts and secure with flat washers and nuts.

◆ To complete the beam, cut $7\frac{1}{2}$-inch-long spacers from 4-by-4 post lumber. Nail the spacers between the boards at 12- to 18-inch intervals, flush with the top and bottom edges.

◆ Build a similar beam on the other two posts.

3. Installing the rafters.

◆ Measure and mark rafter positions on top of the beams at 18- to 24-inch intervals, then cut 1-by-6 boards for the rafters.

◆ Set each rafter on edge across the beams, aligned with the marks and overhanging the beams equally on each side. Toenail the rafters to the beams *(right)*, or use galvanized rafter ties *(inset)*. To prevent splits from occurring when toenailing along the edge of a board, drill pilot holes at the correct angle slightly smaller than the diameter of the nails.

Among vines, there are eager climbers and reluctant ones. You can coax up plants such as climbing rose, which despite its name is not a natural climber, by carefully weaving their stems through a supporting trellis or by tying their stems with string or wire to a support.

However, the classic climbers are a different matter. Provided modest assistance, they will ascend a wall with little further attention. You can buy vines in flats and plant them as you would ground covers *(pages 51-52)*, or you can carefully detach established vines from their support as shown at right and move them to a new location.

Ivy and Brick Walls: Climbing ivy and other clingers *(below)* may compromise weak mortar in a brick wall, allowing moisture to penetrate and weaken the wall's structural integrity. Perform this test: Scratch a key against the joint. If the mortar does not scrape off or crumble, your wall can support the growth.

Caring for Climbers: Periodic pruning will keep vines bushy and robust. Climbers are generally less vulnerable to pests and disease than are low-growing plants. An occasional hosing down of the leaves helps to discourage insects. But vines are susceptible to heat scorch and drought stress from excessive evaporation from the leaves. Water them more often than low-growing varieties. Many vines tolerate frost poorly. Check with a nursery for varieties suitable to your climate.

Three ways vines hold on.
Clingers, such as English ivy and Virginia creeper *(above, left),* anchor themselves even to vertical surfaces with adhesive disks, tiny hooks, or rootlets. Moisture at anchor points can damage wood siding.

Stem twiners *(center)* encircle downspouts, trellises, wires, and strings. Some, such as Hall's Japanese honeysuckle, wrap their stems counterclockwise; others, like Dutchman's pipe, twine in a clockwise direction.

Tendril twiners, including plants like the sweet pea *(right)* and trumpet vine, extend threadlike spirals that wrap tightly around a thin support, such as a wire fence. Some tendril twiners also wind their stems around the support.

EASY UPKEEP FOR CLIMBERS

Thinning a climber.
Prune a climbing plant in summer to improve air circulation and to permit new growth to strengthen the plant before the autumn frost. Clip and disentangle enough large stems (up to $1\frac{1}{4}$ inches in diameter) near ground level to allow light to reach all the inner branches. Prune other areas of the plant selectively, removing unhealthy stems without damaging sound ones.

Encouraging new growth.

To induce lateral buds to sprout new shoots where leaves might otherwise appear, prune stems just above the buds.

In general, vines that flower in the spring bloom on the previous year's growth; prune them after they bloom to give the new growth time to strengthen before winter. Those that flower in late summer or fall bloom on the current year's growth and are best pruned in late autumn when the plant is dormant or in early spring before any new growth appears.

Detaching vines from their support.

When transplanting a clinger, tug gently near the adhesive disks, hooks, or rootlets that grip a wall *(near right)*. Unravel the tendrils or unhook the leaf stalks of a twiner that attaches to a string or wire *(far right)*. When unwinding the stems or tendrils, note whether they grow clockwise or counterclockwise, then wrap them in the appropriate direction around supports at the new location.

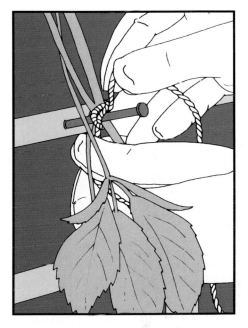

Tethering newly planted vines.

To secure a clinging vine to a brick wall, hammer masonry nails into the mortar joints at 2-foot intervals. Loosely tie the stems of the plant to the nails with string or twist ties *(left)*.

For twiners, stretch string or wire between two nails to provide vertical supports for new growth to climb. Secure the plant stem loosely to the support.

Check the plant periodically, trimming back any yellowed or wilted leaves near the top. When the plant can support itself, remove the strings or ties.

Rock Gardens: Unusual Settings for Unusual Plants

A rock garden can be a handsome addition to many a landscaping plan. Featuring artfully arranged stones and uncommon plants usually found only at high altitudes, rock gardens thrive in a variety of light conditions and require little maintenance.

Choosing a Location: Since alpine plants prefer relatively dry soil, slopes offer the best chance of success because of the superior drainage there. Choose an east-facing slope over a northern exposure, and avoid southern and western slopes; they receive too much warmth for alpine species.

A Matter of Character: A rock garden can mimic the geology of any area, but rather than importing stones from afar, a simpler approach is to imitate local surroundings. Flat, jagged hunks of sandstone may define the character of a rock garden design in one region; in another, granite boulders may predominate. In any case, emphasize large stones, and intersperse smaller ones among them.

The character of a rock garden depends as much on plant selection as on the kind of rock used. Choose from among the alpine varieties offered on page 124 or visit your local nursery for assistance.

Heavy Work: Preparing a rock garden for planting involves a fair amount of labor. Even an incline's superior drainage needs improving before you can set rocks into the slope *(opposite),* singly or as outcrops—stacks of two or more. Tips for maneuvering heavy objects appear on page 19, but don't hesitate to contact a landscaping company to help with the largest stones.

⚠ **CAUTION** *Before excavating, note the location of underground obstacles such as electric, water, and sewer lines, or dry wells, septic tanks, and cesspools.*

TOOLS

Long-handled spade
Trowel
Digging bar

MATERIALS

Large and small rocks
Sand
Compost or peat
Crushed stone
Alpine plants, shrubs, and trees

Anatomy of a rock garden.

The most attractive rock gardens mimic a natural-appearing environment of rocks and plants in an aesthetically pleasing way without seeming studied or fussy. When designing the garden, consider each plant's growth habits, blooming schedule, height, and light requirements. Then, place plants in the setting you have created as they might grow in the wild.

A ROCK GARDEN ON A SLOPE

1. Preparing the bed.

◆ Strip the sod from the site and remove about 18 inches of soil.

◆ In the bottom of the hole, spread a 6-inch layer of rocks or broken bricks, covered by the sod, placed grass side down *(left)*. If there was no sod, cover the rocks and bricks with smaller stones or coarse sand.

◆ Mix 2 parts of coarse sand to 1 part each of the soil from the bed, compost or peat, and crushed stone. Fill the hole to ground level with the mixture.

2. Setting large rocks.

◆ Arrange the rocks atop the soil mixture in the desired locations.

◆ Starting at the bottom of the slope, cut a step deep enough to accommodate at least one-third the width of the first rock. Make the back of the step lower than the front so that rainwater will run toward the slope.

◆ Place the rock into the step with the long side parallel to the slope *(right)*.

◆ Pack soil mixture around the rock, filling any air pockets. Stand on the rock to test its stability.

◆ Repeat for each large rock.

3. Building a rock outcrop.

Where an outcrop is desired, use one of the rocks set in Step 2 as a base. Select large stones that match the appearance of the base rock so that when finished the outcrop resembles a natural formation.

◆ Cover the base rock with an inch of soil and position another rock on top of it. Use a digging bar—a long metal tool helpful for gaining leverage, available at garden centers—to maneuver heavy specimens *(right)*.

◆ Repeat this process to add stones to the outcrop.

Creating Walkways for a Yard

Aesthetically, a walkway can draw the eye to a focal point in the yard. Practically, it can prevent a much trodden path from becoming a sea of mud after rain or snow. Timbered terraces or steps in a walkway not only tame modestly undulating terrain but also can protect a footpath from erosion.

Stepping Stones: For seldom or occasionally traveled routes, flagstones, thin precast concrete slabs, or other kinds of stepping stone can make an attractive walkway. Choose elements that are 18 inches to 24 inches across. Lay rectangular slabs in pairs to form squares, as shown below.

Loose Pavings: For pathways that get more frequent usc, a path of pine needles, bark mulch, or gravel is more suitable. Moreover, loose paving is easier and less expensive to build with than is concrete or brick. Spreading plastic sheeting called landscaping fabric under the paving keeps weeds at bay, and an edging of bricks prevents the paving material from washing into the lawn. Make the path at least 4 feet across, wide enough for two people to walk abreast.

Dealing with Slopes: For gentle inclines, construct a series of terraces called ramps. Set pressure-treated 6-by-8s into the slope and spread loose paving material between them. The distance between timbers can vary from 4 feet to 10 feet; generally, the steeper the slope, the closer together the timbers should be set. Whatever the distance, keep it uniform to help reduce the risk of stumbles.

On slopes too steep for ramps, timber steps make an attractive alternative. They require a hill that allows a tread depth of 11 inches or more *(page 103, Step 1)*. A steeper hill would demand an impractical amount of excavation.

Before beginning, check local building codes; in some jurisdictions, stairways of more than four steps require a handrail.

TOOLS

Edge cutter	Electric drill with
Spade	$\frac{1}{2}$-inch bit
Sod cutter	4-pound maul
Garden rake	Tamper
Line level	Sledgehammer

MATERIALS

Stepping stones	$\frac{1}{2}$-inch steel rein-
Sand	forcing rods
Stakes and string	$\frac{3}{8}$-inch galvanized
Landscaping fabric	spikes
Bricks	6-by-6 and 6-by-8
Loose paving	pressure-treated
	timbers

SAFETY TIPS

Gloves protect your hands during spadework, and a back brace can reduce the risk of injury when digging. Wear goggles whenever you use a hammer.

A CHAIN OF STEPPING STONES

1. Laying out the stones.
◆ Position the stepping stones along the proposed pathway. Adjust them as necessary so that they fall naturally underfoot as you walk the path.
◆ Cut around the stones with an edge cutter *(left)*, then set the stones aside. Remove the sod with a spade, digging $\frac{1}{2}$ inch deeper than the thickness of the stepping stones.

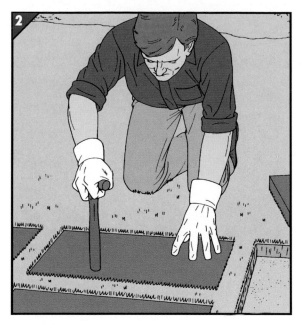

2. Tapping the stones down.

◆ Spread $\frac{1}{2}$ inch of sand in each hole, then place the stones on the sand.
◆ Tap the stones into place with the butt of a hammer *(left)* to bring the tops level with the ground.

PATHS OF GRAVEL OR MULCH

1. Digging the path.

◆ Lay out a straight path with strings and stakes; for a curved path, use a rope or garden hose. Strip the sod between the marks with a sod cutter, then remove 2 or 3 inches of soil with a spade. Smooth the path with a rake.
◆ Dig edging trenches 2 inches wide and 2 inches deeper than the path.
◆ Spread landscaping fabric across the path and into the edging trenches *(above)* to curb weed growth.

2. Edging the path with brick.

◆ Place bricks on end in the trenches on either side *(inset)*. Pack soil behind and under the bricks as needed to align the tops just above grass level.
◆ Fill the path with loose material, then level it with a rake *(above)*.

TERRACES FOR A GENTLE SLOPE

1. Setting the timbers.

◆ Drill three $\frac{1}{2}$-inch pilot holes through the narrow face of a 6-by-8 timber, one in the center and the others 6 inches from each end.

◆ At the bottom of the slope, dig a trench 2 inches deep and set the timber in it *(right)*. Save the displaced soil to use for fill.

◆ With a 4-pound maul, drive 24-inch reinforcing rods through the pilot holes to anchor the timber.

◆ Working up the slope, anchor a timber in a 2-inch-deep trench at each timber location.

2. Making the ramps.

◆ Distribute the dirt from each trench along the uphill side of the corresponding timber. Tamp the loose fill *(right),* retaining a slight slope to the ramp to aid drainage.

◆ Uphill from each timber, spread a layer of loose paving. Keep the top of the layer below the top of the timber, and extend it up the slope to the next timber.

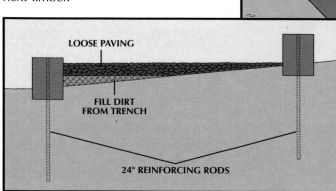

LOOSE PAVING

FILL DIRT
FROM TRENCH

24" REINFORCING RODS

BUILDING TIMBER STEPS

1. Measuring rise and run.
◆ Drive vertical stakes at the top and bottom of the incline. Tie a string to the upper stake at ground level.

◆ Hold the string against the lower stake, and level it with a line level. Mark the lower stake at the string *(right)*, then measure the total rise, that is, the distance in inches between the mark and the ground.

◆ Divide the length of the rise by $5\frac{1}{2}$ inches—the thickness of a 6-by-6 timber—to determine the number of steps. Round a fraction to the nearest whole number.

◆ Next, measure the horizontal distance between the stakes to get total run. Divide the run by the number of steps to find tread depth.

LINE LEVEL

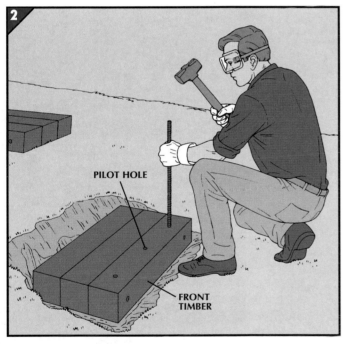

PILOT HOLE

FRONT TIMBER

2. Anchoring the first step.
◆ To make the steps, cut 6-by-6 timbers to the desired width of the stairway. Nail two timbers together with two 10-inch galvanized spikes. Nail additional timbers to one or both sides of the first two to make a step of the correct tread depth, allowing for an overlap of at least 2 inches between steps. Make as many steps as needed for the stairway.

◆ In the front timber of each step, drill three $\frac{1}{2}$-inch pilot holes, one in the center and the others 6 inches from each end.

◆ Working uphill from the stake driven at the bottom of the slope in Step 1, excavate a flat area large enough for the step. Secure the step with 24-inch reinforcing rods as shown above.

3. Installing the second step.
◆ Excavate an area above the first step large enough for the second one and set it in place. With light blows from a sledgehammer *(above)*, adjust the position of the second step to the desired tread depth and step overlap.

◆ Next, drill three $\frac{1}{2}$-inch pilot holes through the steps where they overlap. Drive reinforcing rods through the two steps and into the ground.

◆ Continue overlapping and securing the steps to the top of the slope.

A Pool and Water Garden

Creating a pool and water garden is a big undertaking, but the reward—a dramatic focal point for your yard and a habitat for fish and exotic plants—is substantial. Furthermore, once the pool is completed, upkeep is not any more strenuous than for a traditional flower bed.

New Materials to Line the Pool: Garden pools once were made either of one-piece rigid fiberglass or poured concrete. Nowadays the material of choice is polyvinyl chloride (PVC) plastic or a synthetic rubber called EPDM. With a life of a decade or more, these pliable membranes conform to any pool shape, from geometric to a free-form outline that is meant to mimic a natural pond.

Pool liners are available in a variety of thicknesses; 45 mils (a mil is $\frac{1}{1,000}$ inch) should be sufficient for a backyard pool. When you purchase the liner, it will come folded and boxed and is ready to set in the excavation.

Choosing the Proper Site: Since the banks of the pool must be level all around, select a location on nearly flat terrain. To ensure sunlight for plants and fish, avoid placing the pool directly under a tree.

Some jurisdictions require a fence around pools, usually if they are more than 18 inches deep. Check your local building codes before you break ground.

Finishing Touches: To protect the liner from direct sunlight where it extends above the water line, trim the pool with a coping of flat, thin landscaping stones that overhang the edge. Unless you expect the pool area to receive heavy foot traffic, there is no need to set the stones in mortar.

A pump and fountain not only add a decorative touch to your pool but also will prevent insects from breeding on the pool's surface by keeping the water in motion. Select a fountain head and length of plastic piping in order to create the spray effect that you desire on the surface of the pool.

To power the pump, tap an electrical circuit in the house and extend it to the pool with UF (underground feeder) cable of the same gauge as that of the house circuit. Protect against shock with an outlet containing a ground-fault circuit interrupter (GFCI) *(pages 108-109)*. Alternatively, have an electrician run a new circuit protected by a GFCI in the service panel.

Flora and Fauna: Before stocking a pool, treat the water with a liquid dechlorinating agent available from pool suppliers. Since plants in containers need shallow water, either dig the pool with a 9-inch shelf around the perimeter or stand the containers on concrete blocks.

> ⚠️ **CAUTION** *Before excavating, note the locations of underground obstacles—electric, water, and sewer lines, or dry wells, septic tanks, and cesspools.*

TOOLS

Tape measure
Powdered chalk
Shovel
Wheelbarrow

Edge cutter
Spade
Carpenter's level
Garden rake
Scissors
Push broom
Electric drill

MATERIALS

Ropes or hoses
Lengths of 2-by-4
Sand
Pool liner

Landscaping stones
Dechlorinating agent
10-inch galvanized
   spikes
UF electrical cable
Conduit, nipple, elbow,
   and bushings

LB fitting
Metal strap
Concrete block
Outdoor outlet box
GFCI receptacle

Length/Width of Pool	2 x Depth of Pool	Length/Width of Liner
_____ +	_____ + 4 =	_____ feet

Calculating liner dimensions.

Use the length and width of your pool in feet with the formula above to determine the size liner required. Apply the formula twice, once to find liner length and again for the width. Ignore any shelf you have planned for the pool perimeter; it does not affect the results.

EXCAVATING THE POOL

1. Marking the dimensions.
◆ Outline the shape of your pool on the ground with a rope or hose. Then lay a second rope or hose 1 foot outside the first to mark the strip of sod to be removed for a stone coping.
◆ Measure across the pool outline at its longest and widest points *(right)*, then use the formula on page 104 to calculate the size of the liner you need.
◆ Squeeze powdered chalk from a chalk bottle along both markers, then lift them away.

POOL OUTLINE

SOD LINE

2. Preparing the hole.
◆ Starting at the center of the pool outline, excavate to the desired depth—plus 2 inches for a layer of sand on the bottom. For a shelf, leave a ledge 1 foot wide about 9 inches below ground level. At the pool perimeter, slope the sides of the hole and any shelf about 20 degrees.
◆ Cut along the sod line with an edge cutter *(left)*, then remove the sod inside the line with a spade.

SHELF

3. Leveling the banks.
◆ Rest the ends of a 2-by-4 on opposite banks, inside the sod line.
◆ Level the board, if necessary, by removing soil from the higher bank. Mark the banks under the 2-by-4 with chalk.
◆ Leaving one end of the board on one of the marks, set the other end on the bank at a third point. Add or remove soil there to level the board, then mark that spot with chalk.
◆ Repeat this procedure to level several other points along the banks, always keeping one end of the 2-by-4 on a point that you have already leveled.
◆ Add or remove soil between these points to bring the entire bank to the same height.

4. Checking the depth.

◆ For a level pool bottom, mark the desired depth on a scrap of wood to use as a guide. If the pool will have a shelf, add a second mark to the depth guide 9 inches below the first.

◆ Lay a 2-by-4 across the excavation and hold the depth guide vertically against the 2-by-4 *(left)*, checking at several points for high and low spots. Use the 9-inch mark at the shelves. Add or remove soil to level the shelves and the bottom.

◆ Repeat at various points that span the hole.

5. Preparing the bottom.

Shovel sand into the hole to cushion the pool liner. With a garden rake, spread the sand across the bottom in an even layer 2 inches thick. Do not sand the shelf.

LAYING OUT A PLASTIC OR RUBBER LINER

1. Spreading the liner.

◆ Place the liner in the hole and begin unfolding it, working toward the banks.

◆ With a helper, contour the liner over shelves and up the sides *(left)*. Avoid overlapping folds in the liner and make sure it covers the sod line.

◆ Temporarily anchor the liner with coping stones set at several places around the edge.

◆ Fill the pool with a garden hose. Shifting anchor stones as necessary, smooth the liner so that the rising water presses it flat against the sides.

◆ Add dechlorinating agent according to the manufacturer's directions.

2. Securing the liner.

◆ When the pool is full, trim the liner along the sod line with a pair of scissors *(right)*.

◆ To permanently anchor the liner use a hammer to drive 10-inch galvanized spikes into the banks 4 inches inside the sod line, every 2 feet around the perimeter.

3. Laying the coping.

◆ Place the pump in the pool and run the power cord onto the bank where you plan to install the outlet.

◆ Spread 2 inches of damp sand between the sod line and the pool edge.

◆ Set the coping stones in the sand around the perimeter of the pool so that they extend at least 1 inch over the edge *(below)*, protecting the liner from deterioration caused by sunlight.

◆ Sweep sand into the gaps between stones with the push broom.

1. An exit from the house.

◆ Dig a trench from your house to the receptacle location. Make the trench 6 inches deep if you plan to install rigid metal conduit for the electrical cable; otherwise make it 12 inches deep. Widen the trench near the pool to fit a concrete block.

◆ Drill a $\frac{7}{8}$-inch hole through the house siding and floor framing to accommodate a $\frac{1}{2}$-inch-diameter nipple, a short length of threaded conduit.

◆ To the back of an LB fitting, a small box used to direct cable toward the trench, screw a nipple long enough to extend into the basement or crawlspace (left).

◆ To the other end of the LB fitting, fit a length of conduit that reaches at least 6 inches into the trench. Screw a plastic bushing to the bottom of the conduit.

◆ Push the nipple through the hole into the house and secure the conduit to the foundation with a metal strap.

◆ Inside the house, screw a bushing onto the nipple.

2. Making connections.

◆ Remove the cover plate and gasket of the LB fitting.

◆ Thread UF cable up the conduit and into the LB fitting, then push it through the nipple (left).

◆ At a convenient location inside the house, install a box for a single-pole switch. Run the UF cable to the box, then continue the circuit with indoor (NM) cable, preferably to an existing receptacle.

◆ At the switch, connect black wires to the switch terminals, white wires to each other, and ground wires to the switch and box (if it is metal) by means of jumper wires and wire caps.

Replace the LB fitting's gasket and cover plate, and caulk the joint between fitting and house.

3. Installing the outlet box.

◆ Run cable to the end of the trench.

◆ Screw a bushing to one end of a 12-inch nipple; onto the other, thread an elbow connector. Then cut an 18-inch length of conduit; connect the threaded end to the elbow and the other end to a fitting called a threadless connector (inset).

◆ Thread the cable through this assembly, set it in the trench, and lower a concrete block over it.

◆ Slip a weatherproof outlet box over the cable end and screw it to the threadless connector (right).

◆ Pack soil mixed with stones around the conduit within the concrete block to prevent wobbling, then fill the trench.

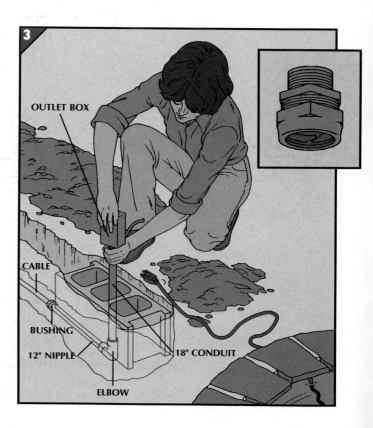

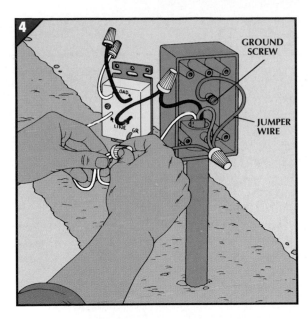

4. Connecting a GFCI receptacle.

◆ Cover both GFCI leads marked LOAD with wire caps.

◆ Connect the black and white wires in the cable to the GFCI wires of corresponding colors marked LINE *(left).*

◆ Attach a jumper wire to the ground screw in the box and join the jumper to cable and GFCI ground wires.

◆ Fold all the wires into the box, screw the outlet in place, and attach a weatherproof GFCI cover.

◆ In the house, turn off power to the receptacle where you intend to tap a circuit. Connect the wires in the new cable to those in the box there, black to black, white to white, and ground to ground.

◆ After screwing the receptacle to the box, restore power, and then plug in the pump.

Maintaining a Healthy Pool

Fish and plants work together to keep your pool clean and attractive. Aquatic plants provide oxygen and food for the fish, which in turn help keep the water clear by feeding on algae.

Periodic Cleaning: Drain your pool and scrub the liner every 3 to 4 years, or after an inch of silt has built up on the bottom. To empty the pool, lift out the plant containers, replace the fountain attachment on the pump with a hose leading outside the pool, then turn on the pump.

When about 6 inches of water remain, remove the fish with a net and place them in a clean plastic container (a new trash can works nicely) with water from the pool. Finish draining the pool, then disconnect the hose and put the pump in the fish container. Run the pump; doing so provides oxygen for the fish. Place the fish and plants in a shaded area.

Gently scrub the liner with a nylon-bristle broom, then use a wet-or-dry vacuum to suck the silt from the pool. Refill the pool and dechlorinate the water. When the pool temperature rises to within 5° of the water temperature in the container, net the fish into the pool and return plants to the shelf.

Winterizing a Pool: When the pool's water temperature drops to 45° F., trim plants to a height of 3 inches and move them from the shelf to the bottom of the pool.

Fish can survive the winter without food, but not without oxygen that enters the water through the surface. In regions with mild winters, water circulation from the pump may prevent the pool from freezing. Should the surface freeze over, however, you must cut in the ice an opening of at least 1 square foot. In extremely cold areas, an electric pond deicer can keep a corner of a pool ice free.

Appendix

Every grass, plant, tree, and shrub has characteristics that best suit it to one environment or another. The charts beginning on page 112, coded to appropriate climatic zone maps, highlight important factors to consider when deciding what to plant. Consult the checklist on the opposite page to schedule planting and landscape maintenance throughout the year.

Year-Round Yard Care

A Checklist of Seasonal Chores

Grasses for Any Climate

Northern Grasses
Southern Grasses
A Map of Grass Zones

Ground Covers

Evergreen
Deciduous
Semievergreen

Yard and Garden Trees

Deciduous
Narrow-Leaved Evergreen
Broad-Leaved Evergreen

Garden Shrubs

Flowering
Evergreen

Plants for Rock Gardens

Flowering

A Map of Minimum Temperatures

YEAR-ROUND YARD CARE

A landscaped yard requires constant attention to stay healthy and beautiful, and each season calls for its own set of chores. Because climates vary widely in the United States, the calendar is an unreliable guide to the seasons. Changes in temperature, soil conditions, and plant appearance are more trustworthy indicators.

The last hard frost marks the beginning of spring, when bulbs begin to put out shoots and perennials unfurl new leaves and stems. Rising soil temperature is a signal for preemptive weed control. Agricultural extension agencies monitor soil temperatures and can tell you other ways they affect landscaping in your area.

Many flowering shrubs bloom in mid-spring, but rosebuds announce the arrival of summer. In northern climes, cooler nighttime temperatures and falling leaves signal the start of autumn. The first few killing frosts are a prelude to winter, when most plants are dormant and require little more than protection from ice and snow.

A Checklist of Seasonal Chores

EARLY SPRING

✓ Remove protective coverings from shrubs and plants. Remove old mulch or mix it into the soil and lay new mulch; start pruning shrubs, trees, and roses.

✓ Rake leaves from the lawn and ground covers. Reseed bare spots in the lawn, spread fertilizer, and water it. Cut grass as low as recommended (page 112), and begin crab grass control by applying a pre-emergent weed-killer.

✓ Fertilize ground covers, and cut away any stringy top growth.

✓ Spray trees and shrubs with a dormant-oil spray for pest control.

MIDSPRING

✓ Cut the grass to a medium height; weed both lawn and garden weekly.

✓ When the soil is moist and easy to work, you can plant or transplant most trees and shrubs.

✓ Edge plant beds; start a vegetable garden.

LATE SPRING

✓ Prune shrubs that do not flower or that will flower in late summer or fall. Prune spring-blooming shrubs after they have lost their blossoms.

✓ Check the lawn periodically to see if the soil needs more or less water.

EARLY SUMMER

✓ Apply pesticides as needed to control fungus, insects, disease, and scale on any plants that have these afflictions. Continue spraying or dusting roses once a week until the growing season ends.

✓ If you have a pool, this is a good time to plant delicate water flowers, such as water lilies and lotuses.

MIDSUMMER

✓ Keep all plants watered well—especially any trees and shrubs planted in the spring—to prevent sunscorched leaves.

✓ Weed flower beds and shrub beds.

✓ Cut grass about 1 inch longer than its springtime length, to prevent burnout.

LATE SUMMER

✓ Start a new lawn or renovate an old one.

✓ Examine plants for possible iron deficiency: If you see yellow leaves with dark green veins, feed the plants with an iron-rich fertilizer.

EARLY FALL

✓ Aerate and dethatch the lawn; cut it shorter and at less frequent intervals.

✓ Dig up and move evergreen shrubs and trees or plant new ones. Wait until the leaves fall before moving deciduous plants.

✓ Plant bare-rooted roses. Water new plants regularly and mulch them lightly to deter weeds.

✓ Fall is an excellent time to start a compost pile; use yard waste such as vegetable tops, dead or dying annuals, and fallen leaves.

✓ Deep-feed tree roots.

LATE FALL

✓ Clear leaves from lawns and ground covers. Rake up pine needles and spread them as mulch for shrubs.

✓ Give roses, trees, and hedges a final pruning.

✓ Renew or replenish mulch on all shrubs. Break up any old, compacted mulch to allow air and water to reach the roots.

✓ Add dead plants from the vegetable garden to the compost pile. Spread manure or compost in the garden, then turn the soil.

✓ Until freezing temperatures set in, water plants well one morning a week to give them moisture to weather the winter.

EARLY WINTER

✓ Cover low shrubs with evergreen clippings; wrap medium-sized shrubs with burlap. Build a shelter over the plants that are near your house, to shield the branches from snow sliding off the roof (page 63).

✓ Trim hollies and other broad-leaved evergreens.

✓ Rake leaves from lawns and flower beds.

MIDWINTER

✓ Check and repair protective coverings often and, after each snowstorm, gently shake the snow from shrub branches.

✓ Take care not to shovel snow onto plants bordering walks and driveways.

✓ After bad storms, cut broken shrub and tree branches. On mild days, finish pruning trees and shrubs that flowered in the late summer and fall.

GRASSES FOR ANY CLIMATE

This chart divides grasses into northern (cool season) and southern (warm season) varieties, each listed by common English name followed by botanical name. Details in the chart include: areas in which each grass grows best, keyed to the map on the facing page; the optimal range of soil pH *(pages 28-29)*; the planting methods and preferred planting seasons; the amount of seed in pounds needed to sow an area of 1,000 square feet; and the ideal mowing height. The last column lists important attributes and the maintenance requirements of each variety.

Northern grasses	ZONES	SOIL PH	PLANTING	SEEDING DENSITY	MOWING HEIGHT	CHARACTERISTICS
Bent grass; colonial, creeping, red top, velvet AGROSTIS	3	5.3-7.5	seed, sprig, sod in fall	1.5-2	$\frac{3}{4}$ inch	*Thick, fine texture; shiny green; grows in cool, humid climates; needs constant maintenance; water frequently, fertilize every month; dethatch yearly*
Bluegrass; Canada, Kentucky, rough-stalk POA	1-3	6.0-7.5	seed, sod in fall or early spring	2-4	2-$2\frac{1}{2}$ inches	*Dense, rich green, fine-textured turf; drought resistant and semidormant in warm weather; Kentucky bluegrass also grows in Zone 4*
Fescue; red, tall FESTUCA	2-5 (tall); 1-3 (red)	5.3-7.5	seed, sod in fall or early spring	6-10	2-3 inches	*Tall is tough, medium-textured turf, red is fine textured, shade tolerant; forms clumps if too sparsely sown; very low maintenance*
Ryegrass; annual, perennial LOLIUM	2-4	5.5-8.0	seed in late fall	6-8	$1\frac{1}{2}$-2 inches	*Fast-growing, light green annual; good for overseeding southern grasses before winter in Zones 5 and 6*
Wheatgrass; crested, western AGROPYRON	2, 4	6.0-8.5	seed in fall or early spring	1-2	2-3 inches	*Bluish green bunches; dormant in summer and tolerant of drought; avoid overwatering and over-fertilizing*

Southern grasses	ZONE(S)	SOIL PH	PLANTING	SEEDING DENSITY	MOWING HEIGHT	CHARACTERISTICS
Bahia grass PASPALUM	6	5.0-6.5	seed, sod in spring	4-6	$2\frac{1}{2}$-3 inches	*Light green, extremely coarse, drought resistant*
Bermuda grass CYNODON	4-6	5.2-7.0	seed, sprig, plug, sod in late spring or summer	2-3	$\frac{1}{2}$-$1\frac{1}{2}$ inches	*Dense, lush, quick spreading; dark green to bluish, depending on hybrid; dethatch each spring*
Blue grama grass BOUTELOUA	2, 4, 5	6.0-8.5	seed in early spring	1-2	2-$2\frac{1}{2}$ inches	*Drought-resistant, small, grayish leaves, which form low tufts*
Buffalo grass BUCHLOE	2, 4, 5	6.0-8.5	seed, plug, sod in spring or summer	3-6	1-$2\frac{1}{2}$ inches	*Rugged, slow-growing, grayish blades, which make a very smooth-textured lawn; may be left unmowed*

KENTUCKY BLUEGRASS

WESTERN WHEATGRASS

BERMUDA GRASS

BUFFALO GRASS

ZOYSIA

Southern, *continued*	ZONES	SOIL PH	PLANTING	SEEDING DENSITY	MOWING HEIGHT	CHARACTERISTICS
Carpet grass AXONOPUS	6	4.7-7.0	seed, sprig, plug, sod in spring or early summer	1.5-2.5	1-2 inches	*Rugged, though spotty, light green turf; survives with little maintenance in acidic, sandy, and poorly drained soil and in wet locations*
Centipede grass EREMOCHLOA	4-6	4.0-6.0	seed, sprig, plug, sod in spring or early summer	4-6	2 inches	*Slow, low-growing, low-maintenance grass with yellowish, coarse leaves*
St. Augustine grass STENOTAPHRUM	6	6.0-7.0	seed, sprig, plug in spring or early summer	2-3	1 2 inches	*Coarse, dense, low-growing, bluish turf; dethatch yearly*
Zoysia Also called Manila, Mascarene, Japanese, Korean lawn grass ZOYSIA	2-6	5.5-7.0	seed, plug, sod in spring or early summer	2-3	½-1½ inches	*Dense, slow-growing turf, ranging from coarse grayish to fine moss green. Infrequent watering and fertilizing.*

A MAP OF GRASS ZONES

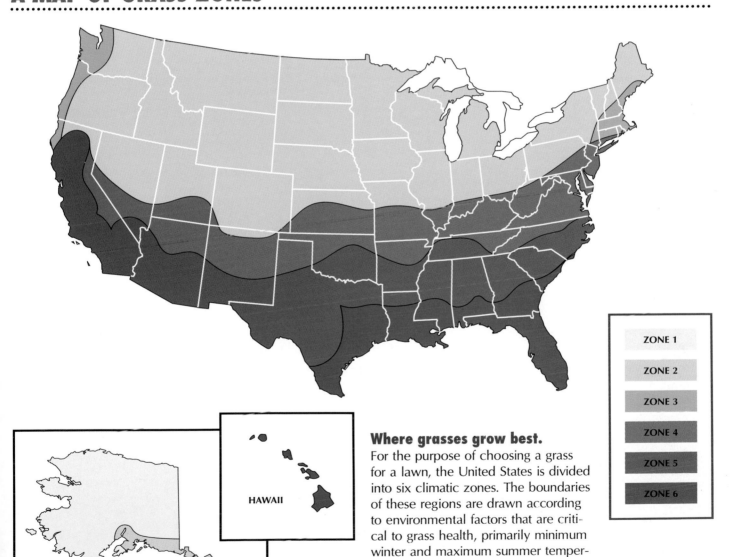

ZONE 1
ZONE 2
ZONE 3
ZONE 4
ZONE 5
ZONE 6

HAWAII

ALASKA

Where grasses grow best.
For the purpose of choosing a grass for a lawn, the United States is divided into six climatic zones. The boundaries of these regions are drawn according to environmental factors that are critical to grass health, primarily minimum winter and maximum summer temperatures and annual rainfall. Northern grasses generally do well in Zones 1 through 4; southern grasses generally prefer Zones 4, 5, and 6.

GROUND COVERS

This chart lists more than three dozen common ground covers by their English and Latin names, grouped according to foliage type—evergreen, deciduous, or semievergreen (plants that keep their leaves only where winters are mild). The zones in which each plant thrives, listed in the second column, are keyed to the map that appears on page 125. Semievergreen plants flourish widely but are green year round only in Zones 8 to 11. Plant height and methods of propagation are listed in the third and fourth columns. The last column notes a variety of special characteristics, such as ground covers that are well suited to slopes or rock gardens and any special light or soil requirements. All of the plants have green foliage and all flower or fruit, unless otherwise noted.

Evergreen	ZONES	HEIGHT	PROPAGATION	SPECIAL CHARACTERISTICS
Bearberry ARCTOSTAPHYLOS UVA-URSI	2-11	8-16"	layering	*Good on slopes; easy maintenance; dry soil*
Candytuft, evergreen IBERIS SEMPERVIRENS	3-11	8-16"	cuttings, division	*Easy maintenance; full sun*
Carmel creeper CEANOTHUS GRISEUS HORIZONTALIS	7-11	over 16"	cuttings	*Good for slopes; full sun*
Coyote brush BACCHARIS PILULARIS	8-11	over 16"	cuttings	*Good for slopes; rapid growth; easy maintenance; full sun*
Daisy, trailing African OSTEOPERMUM FRUTICOSUM	9-11	over 16"	cuttings	*Good for slopes; rapid growth; easy maintenance; full sun; gray-green color*
Dichondra DICHONDRA REPENS	9-11	under 8"	division	*Good for rock gardens; rapid growth; easy maintenance; no flower or fruit*
Geranium, strawberry SAXIFRAGA STOLONIFERA	8-11	under 8"	division, layering	*Rapid growth; easy maintenance; moist soil; partial shade*
Grape, dwarf holly MAHONIA REPENS	5-10	over 16"	cuttings, division	*Good for slopes; rapid growth; easy maintenance; moist soil*
Heath, spring ERICA CARNEA	5-11	over 16"	division, layering	*Good for slopes; moist soil*
Heather, Scotch CALLUNA VULGARIS	4-10	over 16"	cuttings, division	*Good for slopes; easy maintenance; moist soil*
Ivy, English HEDERA HELIX	5-11	under 8"	cuttings	*Good for slopes, rock gardens; rapid growth; easy maintenance; moist soil; vine with no flower or fruit*
Juniper, Wilton carpet JUNIPERUS HORIZONTALIS WILTONII	2-11	under 8"	cuttings	*Good for slopes; easy maintenance; partial shade; no flower or fruit*
Lilyturf, creeping LIRIOPE SPICATA	4-11	8-16"	division	*Easy maintenance*
Pachysandra, Japanese PACHYSANDRA TERMINALIS	4-9	8-16"	cuttings, division	*Good for slopes; rapid growth; easy maintenance; moist soil*
Periwinkle, common VINCA MINOR	4-11	under 8"	cuttings, division	*Vine that is good for slopes; rapid growth; easy maintenance; moist soil; partial shade*
Plum, Green Carpet Natal CARISSA GRANDIFLORA	10-11	8-16"	cuttings	*Moist soil*
Sandwort, moss ARENARIA VERNA SATUREJA	2-11	under 8"	division	*Good for slopes; rapid growth; moist soil*
Snow-in-summer CERASTIUM TOMENTOSUM	2-11	under 8"	cuttings, division	*Good for rock gardens; rapid growth; easy maintenance; full sun; gray-green color*

EVERGREEN CANDYTUFT

TRAILING AFRICAN DAISY

SPRING HEATH

ENGLISH IVY

JAPANESE PACHYSANDRA

Evergreen, *continued*	ZONES	HEIGHT	PROPAGATION	SPECIAL CHARACTERISTICS
Strawberry, sand FRAGARIA CHILOENSIS	8-11	8-16"	cuttings	*Rapid growth; easy maintenance; full sun*
Thrift, common ARMERIA MARITIMA	2-11	8-16"	division	*Good for rock gardens; full sun*
Thyme, wild THYMUS SERPYLLUM	3-11	under 8"	division	*Rapid growth; easy maintenance; dry soil; full sun*
Yarrow, woolly ACHILLEA TOMENTOSA	2-11	8-16"	cuttings, division	*Good for rock gardens; rapid growth; easy maintenance; dry soil; full sun; gray-green color*
Yew, spreading English TAXUS BACCATA	5-11	over 16"	cuttings, layering	*Easy maintenance; moist soil; no flower or fruit*

Deciduous	ZONES	HEIGHT	PROPAGATION	SPECIAL CHARACTERISTICS
Artemesia, Silver Mound ARTEMESIA SCHMIDTIANA	3-11	8-16"	cuttings, division	*Easy maintenance; full sun; gray-green color*
Catmint, mauve NEPETA MUSSINII	4-11	8-16"	cuttings	*Rapid growth; easy maintenance; full sun; gray-green color*
Epimedium EPIMEDIUM GRANDIFLORUM	3-8	8-16"	division	*Easy maintenance; moist soil; partial shade*
Lily of the valley CONVALLARIA MAJALIS	3-7	8-16"	cuttings	*Easy maintenance; moist soil; partial shade*
Rose, Max Graf ROSA 'MAX GRAF'	5-11	over 16"	cuttings, layering	*Easy maintenance; full sun*
Vetch, crown CORONILLA VARIA	3-11	over 16"	division	*Good for slopes; rapid growth; easy maintenance*
Woodruff GALIUM ODORATUM	4-11	8-16"	division	*Rapid growth; easy maintenance; moist soil; partial shade*

Semievergreen	ZONES	HEIGHT	PROPAGATION	SPECIAL CHARACTERISTICS
Baby's-tears SOLEIROLIA SOLEIROLII	9-11	under 8"	cuttings, division	*Rapid growth; easy maintenance; moist soil; partial shade; no flower or fruit*
Bugleweed AJUGA REPTANS	3-11	under 8"	division	*Rapid growth; easy maintenance; moist soil*
Chamomile CHAMAEMELUM NOBILE	3-11	under 8"	division	*Easy maintenance*
Fescue, blue FESTUCA OVINA GLAUCA	3-9	under 8"	division	*Rapid growth; dry soil; full sun; no flower or fruit*
Mint, Corsican MENTHA REQUIENII	6-11	under 8"	division	*Good for rock gardens; rapid growth; moist soil; full sun*
Mondo grass OPHIOPOGON JAPONICUS	8-11	under 8"	division	*Easy maintenance; moist soil*
Phlox, moss PHLOX SUBULATA	3-9	under 8"	cuttings, division	*Good for rock gardens; rapid growth; easy maintenance; full sun*
Rose, memorial ROSA WICHURAIANA	5-11	8-16"	cuttings, layering	*Vine that is good for slopes; rapid growth; easy maintenance; full sun*
St.-John's-wort, Aaron's beard HYPERICUM CALYCINUM	6-11	8-16"	cuttings, division	*Good for slopes; rapid growth; easy maintenance*

MAUVE CATMINT

SILVER MOUND ARTEMESIA

CHAMOMILE

MOSS PHLOX

MONDO GRASS

YARD AND GARDEN TREES

This chart lists 83 small and medium-sized ornamental trees suitable for a garden, patio, or yard; 54 are deciduous, 14 are narrow leafed evergreens, and 15 are broad-leafed evergreens.

The first column gives the common English names of each tree in alphabetical order, followed by the botanical name; the second lists the geographical zone or zones in which each tree grows best *(map, page 125)*. The third column gives the approximate height of a mature tree. Growth rates for trees vary, from less than 12 inches annually (slow), to 1 to 2 feet per year (moderate), to 3 feet or more a year (fast).

Tree shapes sometimes differ within a single species, as listed in the Shape column. The Special Characteristics column includes other qualities, such as striking leaf color or unusual bark, which make trees distinctive; here, too, variations exist within a species. Also noted in this column are soil and sun requirements, and whether a tree produces flowers, fruit, or seeds.

Inquire at a local nursery about trees that are native to your area; these species will flourish, because they have adapted to local conditions.

Deciduous	ZONES	HEIGHT	GROWTH RATE	SHAPE	SPECIAL CHARACTERISTICS
Ash, European mountain SORBUS AUCUPARIA	3-7	over 25 ft.	fast	spreading	*Full sun; flowers; fruit or seeds; colorful leaves*
Ash, Modesto FRAXINUS VELUTINA GLABRA	5-11	over 25 ft.	fast	spreading	*Dry, alkaline soil; full sun; colorful leaves*
Ash, Moraine FRAXINUS HOLOTRICHA 'MORAINE'	5-11	over 25 ft.	fast	columnar, rounded	*Full sun*
Bauhinia, Buddhist BAUHINIA VARIEGATA	10	to 25 ft.	fast	rounded, spreading	*Moist, acidic soil; full sun; flowers; fruit or seeds*
Birch, European white BETULA PENDULA	2-7	over 25 ft.	fast	weeping, conical	*Moist soil; full sun; colorful leaves, attractive bark*
Catalpa, common CATALPA BIGNONIOIDES	5-11	over 25 ft.	fast	rounded	*Flowers; fruit or seeds*
Cherry, double-flowered mazzard PRUNUS AVIUM PLENA	3-8	over 25 ft.	fast	conical	*Full sun; flowers*
Cherry, Higan PRUNUS SUBHIRTELLA	4-9	to 25 ft.	fast	weeping	*Full sun; flowers*
Cherry, paperbark PRUNUS SERRULA	5-6	to 25 ft.	fast	rounded	*Full sun; flowers; fruit or seeds; attractive bark*
Cherry, Yoshino PRUNUS YEDOENSIS	5-8	over 25 ft.	fast	spreading	*Full sun; flowers*
Chestnut, Chinese CASTANEA MOLLISSIMA	4-9	over 25 ft.	fast	spreading	*Acidic soil; full sun; flowers; fruit or seeds; colorful leaves*
Chinaberry MELIA AZEDARACH	7-11	over 25 ft.	fast	rounded	*Alkaline soil; full sun; flowers; fruit or seeds*
Crab apple, Arnold MALUS ARNOLDIANA	4-10	to 25 ft.	moderate	rounded	*Moist, acidic soil; full sun; flowers; fruit or seeds*
Crab apple, Dolgo MALUS 'DOLGO'	3-10	over 25 ft.	moderate	spreading	*Moist, acidic soil; full sun; flowers; fruit or seeds*
Crab apple, Flame MALUS 'FLAME'	2-10	to 25 ft.	moderate	rounded	*Moist, acidic soil; full sun; flowers; fruit or seeds*
Crab apple, Red Jade MALUS 'RED JADE'	4-10	to 25 ft.	moderate	weeping	*Moist, acidic soil; full sun; flowers; fruit or seeds*

EUROPEAN MOUNTAIN ASH

COMMON CATALPA

YOSHINO CHERRY

RED JADE CRAB APPLE

FLOWERING DOGWOOD

Deciduous, *continued*	ZONES	HEIGHT	GROWTH RATE	SHAPE	SPECIAL CHARACTERISTICS
Crab apple, Zumi MALUS ZUMI CALOCARPA	5-10	to 25 ft.	moderate	conical	*Moist, acidic soil; full sun; flowers; fruit or seeds*
Dogwood, flowering CORNUS FLORIDA	5-8	to 25 ft.	moderate	rounded, weeping, spreading	*Moist, acidic soil; full sun; flowers; fruit or seeds; colorful leaves, attractive bark*
Dogwood, Kousa CORNUS KOUSA	4-8	to 25 ft.	moderate	spreading	*Moist, acidic soil; full sun; flowers; fruit or seeds; colorful leaves*
Franklinia FRANKLINIA ALATAMAHA	5-9	to 25 ft.	slow	conical	*Moist, acidic soil; full sun; flowers; colorful leaves*
Fringe tree CHIONANTHUS VIRGINICUS	3-9	to 25 ft.	slow	rounded	*Moist soil; flowers; fruit or seeds; colorful leaves*
Golden-rain tree KOELREUTERIA PANICULATA	5-9	to 25 ft.	fast	rounded	*Alkaline soil; full sun; flowers*
Golden shower CASSIA FISTULA	10-11	to 25 ft.	fast	rounded	*Flowers; fruit or seeds*
Hawthorn, Toba CRATAEGUS MORDENENSIS 'TOBA'	3-10	to 25 ft.	slow	rounded	*Full sun; flowers; fruit or seeds*
Hawthorn, Washington CRATAEGUS PHAENOPYRUM	3-8	over 25 ft.	slow	conical	*Full sun; flowers; fruit or seeds; colorful leaves*
Hop hornbeam, American OSTRYA VIRGINIANA	3-9	over 25 ft.	slow	conical	*Moist soil; flowers; fruit or seeds; colorful leaves*
Hornbeam, European CARPINUS BETULUS	4-8	over 25 ft.	slow	rounded, conical	*Full sun; colorful leaves, attractive bark*
Jacaranda, sharp-leaved JACARANDA ACUTIFOLIA	10-11	over 25 ft.	fast	spreading	*Acidic soil; full sun; flowers; fruit or seeds; attractive bark*
Jerusalem thorn PARKINSONIA ACULEATA	9-11	to 25 ft.	fast	spreading	*Full sun; flowers; fruit or seeds*
Jujube ZIZIPHUS JUJUBA	6-11	to 25 ft.	moderate	spreading	*Alkaline soil; flowers; fruit or seeds*
Katsura tree CERCIDIPHYLLUM JAPONICUM	4-8	over 25 ft.	fast	spreading, conical	*Moist soil; full sun; colorful leaves*
Laburnum, Waterer LABURNUM WATERERI	5-7	to 25 ft.	moderate	rounded	*Moist soil; light shade; flowers*
Lilac, Japanese tree SYRINGA RETICULATA	3-7	to 25 ft.	moderate	spreading	*Moist soil; full sun; flowers*
Locust, Idaho ROBINIA 'IDAHO'	3-11	over 25 ft.	fast	conical	*Dry, alkaline soil; full sun; flowers*
Magnolia, saucer MAGNOLIA SOULANGIANA	4-11	to 25 ft.	moderate	spreading	*Moist, acidic soil; flowers; fruit or seeds; colorful leaves, attractive bark*
Maple, Amur ACER GINNALA	2-8	to 25 ft.	fast	rounded	*Flowers; fruit or seeds; colorful leaves*
Maple, Japanese ACER PALMATUM	5-8	to 25 ft.	slow	rounded	*Moist soil; light shade; colorful leaves*
Maple, paperbark ACER GRISEUM	4-8	to 25 ft.	slow	rounded	*Full sun; colorful leaves, attractive bark*
Maple, vine ACER CIRCINATUM	5-10	to 25 ft.	moderate	spreading	*Moist soil; light shade; flowers; fruit or seeds; colorful leaves*

FRINGE TREE

KATSURA TREE

WASHINGTON HAWTHORN

SAUCER MAGNOLIA

JAPANESE MAPLE

Deciduous, *continued*	ZONES	HEIGHT	GROWTH RATE	SHAPE	SPECIAL CHARACTERISTICS
Mesquite, honey PROSOPIS GLANDULOSA	8-10	over 25 ft.	fast	conical	*Dry, alkaline soil; full sun; flowers; fruit or seeds; attractive bark*
Oak, California black QUERCUS KELLOGGII	7-10	over 25 ft.	moderate	spreading	*Acidic soil; full sun; fruit or seeds; colorful leaves*
Olive, Russian ELAEAGNUS ANGUSTIFOLIA	2-7	to 25 ft.	fast	rounded	*Full sun; flowers; fruit or seeds; colorful leaves, attractive bark*
Parasol tree, Chinese FIRMIANA SIMPLEX	7-11	over 25 ft.	fast	conical	*Moist soil; full sun; flowers; fruit or seeds; attractive bark*
Pear, Bradford PYRUS CALLERYANA 'BRADFORD'	5-9	over 25 ft.	moderate	conical	*Full sun; flowers; fruit or seeds; colorful leaves*
Pistache, Chinese PISTACIA CHINENSIS	6-9	over 25 ft.	fast	rounded	*Alkaline soil; full sun; fruit or seeds; colorful leaves*
Plum, Pissard PRUNUS CERASIFERA ATROPURPUREA	4-8	to 25 ft.	fast	rounded	*Full sun; flowers; fruit or seeds; colorful leaves*
Poinciana, royal DELONIX REGIA	10-11	over 25 ft.	fast	spreading	*Full sun; flowers; fruit or seeds*
Redbud, eastern CERCIS CANADENSIS	3-9	over 25 ft.	moderate	rounded, spreading	*Moist soil; flowers; fruit or seeds; colorful leaves*
Serviceberry, apple AMELANCHIER GRANDIFLORA	4-9	to 25 ft.	fast	rounded	*Moist soil; flowers; colorful leaves*
Silver bell, Carolina HALESIA CAROLINA	4-8	to 25 ft.	slow	rounded, conical	*Moist, acidic soil; flowers; colorful leaves*
Snowbell, Japanese STYRAX JAPONICUS	5-8	to 25 ft.	slow	spreading	*Moist soil; flowers; colorful leaves*
Sorrel tree OXYDENDRUM ARBOREUM	4-9	to 25 ft.	slow	conical	*Moist, acidic soil; full sun; flowers; fruit or seeds; colorful leaves*
Tallow tree, Chinese SAPIUM SEBIFERUM	7-10	over 25 ft.	fast	spreading	*Full sun; fruit or seeds; colorful leaves*
Walnut, Hinds black JUGLANS HINDSII	8-10	over 25 ft.	fast	rounded	*Full sun; fruit or seeds*

Narrow-Leaved Evergreen	ZONES	HEIGHT	GROWTH RATE	SHAPE	SPECIAL CHARACTERISTICS
Arborvitae, Douglas THUJA OCCIDENTALIS DOUGLASII AUREA	2-11	to 25 ft.	fast	conical	*Moist soil; full sun*
Cedar, California incense CALOCEDRUS DECURRENS	5-11	over 25 ft.	fast	conical	*Moist soil; fruit or seeds; attractive bark*
Cedar, Japanese CRYPTOMERIA JAPONICA	5-11	over 25 ft.	fast	conical	*Moist, acidic soil; full sun; fruit or seeds; colorful leaves, attractive bark*
Cypress, Italian CUPRESSUS SEMPERVIRENS STRICTA	7-9	over 25 ft.	fast	columnar	*Dry soil; full sun; fruit or seeds; colorful leaves*
Cypress, moss sawara, false CHAMAECYPARIS PISIFERA SQUARROSA	4-8	over 25 ft.	moderate	conical	*Moist soil; full sun*
Fir, China CUNNINGHAMIA LANCEOLATA	6-9	to 25 ft.	fast	conical	*Acidic soil; fruit or seeds; colorful leaves, attractive bark*
Juniper, blue column JUNIPERUS CHINENSIS COLUMNARIS	3-9	to 25 ft.	moderate	conical	*Dry soil; full sun*

CALIFORNIA BLACK OAK

RUSSIAN OLIVE

PISSARD PLUM

JAPANESE CEDAR

FALSE MOSS SAWARA CYPRESS

Narrow-Leaved, *continued*	ZONES	HEIGHT	GROWTH RATE	SHAPE	SPECIAL CHARACTERISTICS
Pine, Japanese black PINUS THUNBERGIANA	5-11	over 25 ft.	fast	spreading, conical	*Dry soil; full sun; fruit or seeds*
Pine, Norfolk Island ARAUCARIA HETEROPHYLLA	7-11	over 25 ft.	fast	conical	*Moist, acidic soil; full sun; fruit or seeds*
Pine, Tanyosho PINUS DENSIFLORA UMBRACULIFERA	3-7	to 25 ft.	slow	spreading	*Dry soil; full sun; fruit or seeds; colorful leaves*
Pine, umbrella SCIADOPITYS VERTICILLATA	4-11	to 25 ft.	slow	conical	*Moist, alkaline soil; full sun; fruit or seeds*
Podocarpus yew PODOCARPUS MACROPHYLLUS	8-11	to 25 ft.	moderate	columnar	*Moist soil; light shade; colorful leaves*
Spruce, Serbian PICEA OMORIKA	4-7	over 25 ft.	slow	conical	*Full sun; fruit or seeds*
Yew, Irish TAXUS BACCATA STRICTA	5-11	to 25 ft.	slow	columnar, conical	*Acidic soil; fruit or seeds; colorful leaves*

Broad-Leaved Evergreen	ZONES	HEIGHT	GROWTH RATE	SHAPE	SPECIAL CHARACTERISTICS
Ash, shamel FRAXINUS UHDEI 'MAJESTIC BEAUTY'	9-11	over 25 ft.	fast	spreading	*Moist, alkaline soil; full sun*
Camphor tree CINNAMOMUM CAMPHORA	9-11	over 25 ft.	moderate	spreading	*Flowers; fruit or seeds; colorful leaves*
Cootamundra wattle ACACIA BAILEYANA	10-11	to 25 ft.	fast	rounded	*Dry soil; full sun; flowers; colorful leaves*
Elm, Chinese ULMUS PARVIFOLIA	4-11	over 25 ft.	fast	weeping	*Full sun*
Holly, English ILEX AQUIFOLIUM	6-10	over 25 ft.	slow	rounded	*Acidic soil; full sun; fruit or seeds; colorful leaves*
Horsetail beefwood CASUARINA EQUISETIFOLIA	9-11	over 25 ft.	fast	conical	*Fruit or seeds*
Laurel LAURUS NOBILIS	6-11	to 25 ft.	slow	conical	*Fruit or seeds*
Loquat ERIOBOTRYA JAPONICA	8-11	to 25 ft.	fast	spreading	*Moist soil; flowers; fruit or seeds; colorful leaves*
Oleander NERIUM OLEANDER	8-11	to 25 ft.	moderate	rounded	*Moist soil; full sun; flowers*
Olive, common OLEA EUROPAEA	9-11	to 25 ft.	moderate	rounded	*Dry soil; full sun; flowers; fruit or seeds; attractive bark*
Orange, sweet CITRUS SINENSIS	9-11	to 25 ft.	moderate	rounded	*Moist soil; full sun; flowers; fruit or seeds*
Osmanthus, holly OSMANTHUS HETEROPHYLLUS	7-11	to 25 ft.	fast	rounded	*Dry soil; light shade; flowers*
Pepper tree, California SCHINUS MOLLE	9-11	over 25 ft.	moderate	weeping	*Full sun; flowers; fruit or seeds*
Photinia, Fraser PHOTINIA FRASERI	8-11	to 25 ft.	moderate	spreading	*Flowers; fruit or seeds; colorful leaves*
Pineapple guava FEIJOA SELLOWIANA	8-11	to 25 ft.	fast	rounded	*Moist soil; flowers; fruit or seeds; colorful leaves*

OLEANDER

SWEET ORANGE

PINEAPPLE GUAVA

**JAPANESE
BLACK PINE**

**ENGLISH
HOLLY**

GARDEN SHRUBS

This chart lists 58 flowering shrubs by their common English names, followed by their botanical names. The numbered zones in which each shrub can be grown are keyed to the map on page 125. In the chart's third column

the approximate height for each variety is listed. Colored circles in the fourth column indicate the range of flower colors usually produced by each shrub or its relatives. To the right of the colors is the shrub's blooming season. The

Special Characteristics column contains uses to which the plant is well suited—a hedge or a ground cover, for example; its soil and sun preferences; and the presence of fruit, attractive foliage, or a pleasant fragrance.

Flowering	ZONES	HEIGHT	FLOWER COLORS	BLOOMING SEASON	SPECIAL CHARACTERISTICS
Acacia, rose ROBINIA HISPIDA	5-9	to 6 ft.	○●	spring-summer	*Ground cover; full sun*
Almond, flowering PRUNUS TRILOBA	5-9	over 6 ft.	○●	spring	*Full sun; fruit; attractive foliage*
Azalea, catawba RHODODENDRON CATAWBIENSE	3-10	over 6 ft.	○●●●	spring	*Moist, acidic soil; shade*
Azalea, Exbury hybrid RHODODENDRON	5-8	to 6 ft.	○○●●●	summer	*Moist, acidic soil; attractive foliage*
Azalea, flame RHODODENDRON CALENDULACEUM	4-10	to 6 ft.	○●●●	summer	*Moist, acidic soil*
Azalea, pinxter-bloom RHODODENDRON NUDIFLORUM	3-8	to 6 ft.	○●●	spring	*Moist, acidic soil*
Barberry, Japanese BERBERIS THUNBERGII	4-10	over 6 ft.	○●	spring	*Hedge; fruit*
Barberry, Mentor BERBERIS MENTORENSIS	5-10	over 6 ft.	○●	spring	*Hedge; fruit*
Beauty-bush KOLKWITZIA AMABILIS	4-9	over 6 ft.	○●	spring	*Fruit; attractive foliage*
Broom, hybrid CYTISUS HYBRIDS	6-11	any	○○○○●●●	spring	*Full sun; fragrant*
Buckeye, bottlebrush AESCULUS PARVIFLORA	4-10	over 6 ft.	○	summer	*Attractive foliage*
Butterfly bush, fountain BUDDLEIA ALTERNIFOLIA	5-11	over 6 ft.	●●	spring-summer	*Full sun; attractive foliage; fragrant*
Cherry, Cornelian CORNUS MAS	4-8	over 6 ft.	○●	spring	*Fruit; attractive foliage*
Cherry, western sand PRUNUS BESSEYI	3-6	over 6 ft.	○	spring	*Full sun; fruit*
Chokeberry, black ARONIA MELANOCARPA	4-10	under 3 ft.	○●●	spring	*Fruit; attractive foliage*
Chokeberry, brilliant ARONIA ARBUTIFOLIA BRILLIANTISSIMA	4-10	over 6 ft.	○●●	spring	*Fruit; attractive foliage*
Cinquefoil, bush POTENTILLA FRUTICOSA	2-9	to 6 ft.	○○●	summer-fall	*Full sun*

EXBURY HYBRID AZALEA

HYBRID BROOM

CORNELIAN CHERRY

BUSH CINQUEFOIL

JAPANESE BARBERRY

Flowering, *continued*	ZONES	HEIGHT	FLOWER COLORS	BLOOMING SEASON	SPECIAL CHARACTERISTICS
Cotoneaster, early COTONEASTER ADPRESSUS	4-11	under 3 ft.	◯⬤	summer	*Full sun; fruit; attractive foliage*
Cotoneaster, horizontal COTONEASTER HORIZONTALIS	5-11	under 3 ft.	◯⬤⬤⬤	summer	*Ground cover; full sun; attractive foliage*
Cotoneaster, Sungari COTONEASTER RACEMIFLORUS	3-11	over 6 ft.	◯	summer	*Full sun; fruit; attractive foliage*
Crape myrtle LAGERSTROEMIA INDICA	7-10	over 6 ft.	◯◯⬤⬤⬤	summer	*Hedge; moist soil; full sun; attractive foliage*
Daphne, February DAPHNE MEZEREUM	4-9	under 3 ft.	◯⬤	spring	*Fruit; fragrant*
Deutzia, slender DEUTZIA GRACILIS	4-9	to 6 ft.	◯	spring	*Hedge*
Enkianthus, redvein ENKIANTHUS CAMPANULATUS	4-9	over 6 ft.	◯	spring	*Moist, acidic soil; attractive foliage*
Forsythia, border FORSYTHIA INTERMEDIA	5-9	over 6 ft.	◯⬤	spring	*Hedge*
Hazelnut, curly CORYLUS AVELLANA CONTORTA	4-9	over 6 ft.	◯⬤	spring	*Attractive foliage*
Honeysuckle, Amur LONICERA MAACKII	2-9	over 6 ft.	◯	spring	*Fruit; fragrant*
Honeysuckle, Tatarian LONICERA TATARICA	3-9	over 6 ft.	◯◯⬤	spring	*Fruit*
Honeysuckle, winter LONICERA FRAGRANTISSIMA	5-9	to 6 ft.	◯	spring	*Fruit; fragrant*
Hydrangea, peegee HYDRANGEA PANICULATA	4-9	over 6 ft.	◯◯⬤	summer-fall	*Moist soil*
Jasmine, winter JASMINUM NUDIFLORUM	6-9	over 6 ft.	◯⬤	spring	*Full sun*
Kerria KERRIA JAPONICA	4-9	to 6 ft.	◯⬤	spring-summer-fall	*Attractive foliage*
Lilac, common SYRINGA VULGARIS	3-7	over 6 ft.	◯◯⬤⬤⬤⬤	spring	*Fragrant*
Mock orange, Lemoine PHILADELPHUS LEMOINEI	5-9	to 6 ft.	◯	summer	*Fragrant*
Olive, Russian ELAEAGNUS ANGUSTIFOLIA	2-9	over 6 ft.	◯⬤	summer	*Hedge; full sun; fruit; attractive foliage; fragrant*
Pearlbush, common EXOCHORDA RACEMOSA	5-9	over 6 ft.	◯	spring	*Full sun*
Photinia, Oriental PHOTINIA VILLOSA	4-8	over 6 ft.	◯	spring	*Fruit; attractive foliage*
Plum, beach PRUNUS MARITIMA	3-7	to 6 ft.	◯	spring	*Full sun; fruit*
Privet, Amur LIGUSTRUM AMURENSE	3-9	over 6 ft.	◯	summer	*Hedge; fruit*

HORIZONTAL COTONEASTER

CRAPE MYRTLE

KERRIA

COMMON LILAC

LEMOINE MOCK ORANGE

Flowering, continued	ZONES	HEIGHT	FLOWER COLORS	BLOOMING SEASON	SPECIAL CHARACTERISTICS
Privet, Regel LIGUSTRUM OBTUSIFOLIUM	3-9	to 6 ft.	○	summer	*Hedge; fruit*
Privet, vicary golden LIGUSTRUM VICARYI	4-9	over 6 ft.	○	summer	*Hedge; fruit; attractive foliage*
Pussy willow SALIX DISCOLOR	2-9	over 6 ft.	○	spring	*Moist soil; full sun*
Quince, hybrid flowering CHAENOMELES HYBRIDS	6-10	to 6 ft.	○◐●	spring	*Hedge; full sun*
Rose, Japanese ROSA RUGOSA	2-10	to 6 ft.	○◐●	summer-fall	*Full sun; fruit; attractive foliage; fragrant*
Snowberry SYMPHORICARPOS ALBUS	3-9	to 6 ft.	◐●	summer	*Hedge; fruit*
Spirea, bridal-wreath SPIRAEA PRUNIFOLIA	4-10	over 6 ft.	○	spring	*Hedge; attractive foliage*
Spirea, Bumalda SPIRAEA BUMALDA	5-10	under 3 ft.	◐●	summer	*Attractive foliage*
Spirea, Ural false SORBARIA SORBIFOLIA	2-8	to 6 ft.	○	summer	*Moist soil*
Spirea, Vanhoutte SPIRAEA VANHOUTTEI	4-10	to 6 ft.	○	spring	*Hedge*
Summer-sweet CLETHRA ALNIFOLIA	3-10	to 6 ft.	○	summer	*Moist, acidic soil; attractive foliage; fragrant*
Sweet shrub CALYCANTHUS FLORIDUS	4-10	to 6 ft.	◐●	spring	*Moist soil; attractive foliage; fragrant*
Tamarisk, five-stamened TAMARIX PENTANDRA	2-11	over 6 ft.	◐●	summer	*Sun; attractive foliage*
Viburnum, fragrant snowball VIBURNUM CARLCEPHALUM	5-9	over 6 ft.	○	spring	*Hedge; fruit; attractive foliage; fragrant*
Viburnum, Marie's double file VIBURNUM PLICATUM	5-9	over 6 ft.	○	spring	*Hedge; fruit; attractive foliage*
Viburnum, Siebold VIBURNUM SIEBOLDII	4-9	over 6 ft.	○	spring	*Fruit; attractive foliage*
Weigela, hybrid WEIGELA	5-9	to 6 ft.	○◐●	spring	
Winter hazel, fragrant CORYLOPSIS GLABRESCENS	5-9	over 6 ft.	◐◐	spring	*Moist, acidic soil; attractive foliage; fragrant*
Witch hazel, Chinese HAMAMELIS MOLLIS	5-9	over 6 ft.	◐◐	spring	*Moist soil; attractive foliage; fragrant*

PUSSY WILLOW

HYBRID FLOWERING QUINCE

MARIE'S DOUBLE FILE VIBURNUM

HYBRID WEIGELA

CHINESE WITCH HAZEL

This chart lists 20 evergreen shrubs by their common names, then by their botanical names. The numbered zones in which each shrub can be grown refer to the map on page 125. Special characteristics and growing conditions are mentioned in the last column; these include specific uses, such as a lawn specimen, hedge, screen, or ground cover; soil requirements; and whether the plant produces fruit, berries, or flowers.

Evergreen	ZONES	HEIGHT	FOLIAGE COLOR	SPECIAL CHARACTERISTICS
Arbor vitae, Berckman's golden PLATYCLADUS ORIENTALIS	7-11	to 6 ft.	green, yellow-green	*Hedge, screen; moist soil*
Bearberry, 'Point Reyes' ARCTOSTAPHYLOS UVA-URSI 'POINT REYES'	2-11	under 1 ft.	dark green	*Ground cover; dry, acidic soil; fruits or berries; pink-red flowers*
Box, edging BUXUS SEMPERVIRENS SUFFRUTICOSA	5-6	to 3 ft.	blue-green	*Lawn specimen; hedge; moist soil*
Camellia, common CAMELLIA JAPONICA	7-11	to 10 ft.	dark green	*Lawn specimen, hedge; moist, acidic soil; pink-red flowers*
Cypress, false slender hinoki CHAMAECYPARIS OBTUSA	4-8	to 6 ft.	dark green	*Lawn specimen; moist soil*
Cypress, false thread sawara CHAMAECYPARIS PISIFERA	4-8	to 10 ft.	green	*Lawn specimen; moist soil*
Fire thorn, Laland PYRACANTHA COCCINEA	5-11	to 10 ft.	dark green	*Hedge; fruits or berries; white flowers*
Grape, Oregon holly MAHONIA AQUIFOLIUM	4-8	to 6 ft.	green	*Fruits or berries; yellow-orange flowers*
Holly, American ILEX OPACA	5-9	to 10 ft.	green	*Hedge; acidic soil; fruits or berries*
Holly, Burford ILEX CORNUTA	6-9	to 10 ft.	green	*Hedge; acidic soil; fruits or berries*
Holly, Japanese ILEX CRENATA	5-7	to 10 ft.	dark green	*Hedge; acidic soil; fruits or berries*
Juniper, Gold Coast JUNIPERUS CHINENSIS AUREA	3-11	to 3 ft.	yellow-green	*Lawn specimen, ground cover*
Juniper, tamarix JUNIPERUS SABINA	3-11	to 3 ft.	blue-green	*Ground cover*
Juniper, Wilton carpet JUNIPERUS HORIZONTALIS	3-11	under 1 ft.	blue-green	*Ground cover*
Laurel, mountain KALMIA LATIFOLIA	4-9	to 10 ft.	dark green	*Lawn specimen; moist, acidic soil; pink-red flowers*
Nandina NANDINA DOMESTICA	6-11	to 6 ft.	green	*Moist soil; fruits or berries; white flowers*
Pine, Mugo PINUS MUGO	2-8	to 3 ft.	dark green	*Lawn specimen, hedge, ground cover*
Spruce, dwarf Alberta PICEA GLAUCA	2-6	to 10 ft.	blue-green	*Lawn specimen, hedge, screen*
Tea tree LEPTOSPERMUM SCOPARIUM	9-11	to 10 ft.	green	*Hedge; acidic soil; pink-red flowers*
Yew, spreading English TAXUS BACCATA REPANDENS	5-11	to 6 ft.	dark green	*Lawn specimen, hedge; acidic soil*

GOLD COAST JUNIPER

MOUNTAIN LAUREL

LALAND FIRE THORN

DWARF ALBERTA SPRUCE

TEA TREE

PLANTS FOR ROCK GARDENS

In the chart below, plants are listed by their most common English names, followed by their scientific Latin names. The second column indicates the climatic zone or zones in which each plant can be grown, keyed by number to the map at right. All of the plants flower, and a few plants have additional special traits. Bishop's hat, fringed bleeding heart, and leadwort have distinctive foliage, while common thrift is an evergreen. Plant heights, listed in the next column, include the height of the flowers, and the fourth column indicates the blossoms' range of colors. The Growth Habit column shows that most of these plants grow upright, but some grow either by spreading or by trailing from a central stem. Special soil and light conditions in which specific plants thrive appear in the last column.

Flowering	ZONES	HEIGHT	FLOWER COLORS	GROWTH HABIT	SOIL AND LIGHT
Anemone, European wood ANEMONE NEMOROSA	3-8	under 6"	○●●●●●	upright	*acidic soil; partial shade*
Basket-of-gold AURINIA SAXATILIS	4	6-12"	○○	spreading	*full sun*
Bishop's hat EPIMEDIUM GRANDIFLORUM	3-8	6-12"	○●○●●●●	upright	*shade*
Bleeding heart, fringed DICENTRA EXIMIA	3-8	over 12"	○○●●	upright	*acidic soil; shade*
Candytuft, evergreen IBERIS SEMPERVIRENS	3-11	6-12"	○●	spreading	*alkaline soil; full sun*
Cheddar plant DIANTHUS GRATIANOPOLITANUS	4	6-12"	○●○●	upright	*full sun*
Foamflower TIARELLA CORDIFOLIA	4	6-12"	○●	upright	*acidic soil; shade*
Goldenstar CHRYSOGONUM VIRGINIANUM	4-8	6-12"	○○	upright, spreading	*acidic soil; shade*
Harebell, Carpathian CAMPANULA CARPATICA	3-8	6-12"	○●●●	upright	*full sun*
Iris, dwarf bearded IRIS PUMILA	5	6-12"	○●○●○●●●	upright	*alkaline soil; full sun*
Iris, dwarf crested IRIS CRISTATA	3-8	under 6"	○●●●	upright	*acidic soil; partial shade*
Leadwort CERATOSTIGMA PLUMBAGINOIDES	6-11	under 6"	●●	spreading	*partial shade*
Phlox, wild blue PHLOX DIVARICATA	4	6-12"	○●●●	spreading	*acidic soil; partial shade*
Pink, wild SILENE CAROLINIANA	6	6-12"	○●	upright	*partial shade*
Primrose, Siebold PRIMULA SIEBOLDII	5	6-12"	○●○●●●	upright	*acidic soil; partial shade*
Rose, sun HELIANTHEMUM NUMMULARIUM	5-9	6-12"	○●○○○●	upright, trailing	*alkaline soil; full sun*
Sandwort, mountain ARENARIA MONTANA	4-11	under 6"	○●	trailing	*acidic soil; full sun*
Soapwort, rock SAPONARIA OCYMOIDES	2-8	6-12"	○●○●	trailing	*full sun*
Thrift, common ARMERIA MARITIMA	4-8	6-12"	○●○●	upright	*full sun*

EUROPEAN WOOD ANEMONE

BASKET-OF-GOLD

EVERGREEN CANDYTUFT

GOLDENSTAR

DWARF BEARDED IRIS

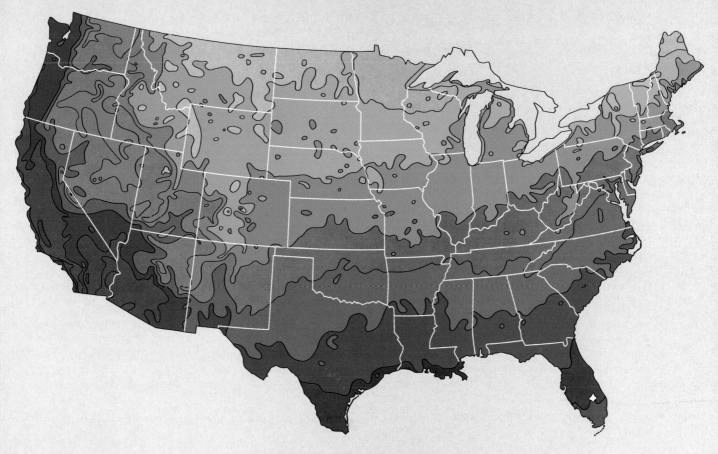

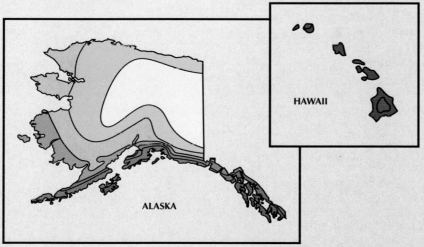

HAWAII

ALASKA

ZONE 1	BELOW -50° F.
ZONE 2	-50° TO -40°
ZONE 3	-40° TO -30°
ZONE 4	-30° TO -20°
ZONE 5	-20° TO -10°
ZONE 6	-10° TO 0°
ZONE 7	0° TO 10°
ZONE 8	10° TO 20°
ZONE 9	20° TO 30°
ZONE 10	30° TO 40°
ZONE 11	ABOVE 40°

Plants and winter cold.

Successful landscaping depends upon a choice of plants that thrive on the land they adorn. Since soil conditions and moisture levels can usually be altered artificially, limitations on where plants will flourish depend largely upon the severity of winter cold. This map devised by the U.S. Department of Agriculture divides the United States into 11 numbered and colored zones, each distinguished by an average minimum winter temperature. Use the charts of ground covers *(pages 114-115)*, flowering shrubs *(pages 120-121)*, and rock-garden plants *(opposite)* with this map to select plants that will grow best in your area.

INDEX

Time-Life Books is a division of Time Life Inc.

PRESIDENT and CEO: John M. Fahey Jr.
EDITOR-IN-CHIEF: John L. Papanek

TIME-LIFE BOOKS

MANAGING EDITOR: Roberta Conlan

Director of Design: Michael Hentges
Director of Editorial Operations:
  Ellen Robling
Director of Photography and Research:
  John Conrad Weiser
Senior Editors: Russell B. Adams Jr.,
  Dale M. Brown, Janet Cave, Lee Hassig,
  Robert Somerville, Henry Woodhead
Special Projects Editor: Rita Thievon Mullin
Director of Technology: Eileen Bradley
Library: Louise D. Forstall

PRESIDENT: John D. Hall

Vice President, Director of Marketing:
  Nancy K. Jones
*Vice President, Director of New Product
  Development:* Neil Kagan
Vice President, Book Production: Marjann
  Caldwell
Production Manager: Marlene Zack
Quality Assurance Manager: James King

HOME REPAIR AND IMPROVEMENT

SERIES EDITOR: Lee Hassig
Administrative Editor: Barbara Levitt

Editorial Staff for *Landscaping*
Art Directors: Kathleen D. Mallow,
  Barbara M. Sheppard
Picture Editor: Catherine Chase Tyson
Text Editor: James Michael Lynch
Associate Editors/Research-Writing:
  Dan Kulpinski, Terrell D. Smith
Technical Art Assistant: Angela Johnson
Senior Copyeditor: Juli Duncan
Copyeditor: Judith Klein
Picture Coordinator: Paige Henke
Editorial Assistant: Amy S. Crutchfield

Special Contributors: John Drummond
  (illustration); William Graves, Craig
  Hower, Marvin Shultz, Eileen Wentland
  (digital illustration); George Constable,
  Chris Hoelzl, J. T. Holland, Brian
  McGinn, Dean Nadalin, Peter Pocock,
  Glen Ruh, Eric Weissman (text); Mel
  Ingber (index).

Correspondents: Christine Hinze (London),
  Christina Lieberman (New York), Maria
  Vincenza Aloisi (Paris), Ann Natanson
  (Rome).

PICTURE CREDITS

Cover: Photograph, Ronnie Luttrell; Art,
Carol Hilliard and Patrick Wilson/Totally
Incorporated.

Illustrators: Jack Arthur, George Bell, Fred-
eric F. Bigio from B-C Graphics, Roger
C. Essley, Donald Gates, Adisai Hem-
intranont from Sai Graphis, William
J. Hennessy Jr., Elsie J. Hennig, Fil
Hunter, John Jones, Arezou Katoozian
from A and W Graphics, Dick Lee,
Jennifer and John Massey, Joan McGur-
ren, Eduino J. Pereira, Graham Sayles,
Stephen Turner, Stephen R. Wagner,
Walter Hilmers Studios.

Photographers: (Credits from left to right
are separated by semicolons, from top to
bottom by dashes.) **End papers:** Renée
Comet. **7, 8, 20:** Renée Comet. **33:** Rain
Bird. **35:** The Toro Company. **38:** L. R.
Nelson Corporation. **39:** L. R. Nelson
Corporation (2)—Renée Comet. **48, 49,
53, 57, 72, 80:** Renée Comet. **83:** Jerry
Pavia. **86, 91:** Renée Comet. **109:** Ron-
nie Luttrell. **112:** Doug Brede. **114:** Jerry
Pavia; Joanne Pavia; Jerry Pavia; Joanne
Pavia; Jerry Pavia. **115:** Jerry Pavia. **116:**
Joanne Pavia; Jerry Pavia (4). **117:** Jerry
Pavia (2); Joanne Pavia (2); Jerry Pavia.
118: Joanne Pavia (3); Jerry Pavia (2).
119: Jerry Pavia (3); Joanne Pavia; Jerry
Pavia. **120, 121:** Jerry Pavia. **122:** Joanne
Pavia (2); Jerry Pavia (3). **123:** Joanne
Pavia; Jerry Pavia (4). **124:** Jerry Pavia
(4); Joanne Pavia.

ACKNOWLEDGMENTS

Christopher Baldwin, Middleburg, Va.; Joe
Beben, Fairfax County Department of Envi-
ronmental Management, Public Utilities
Branch, Fairfax, Va.; Doug Brede, Jacklin
Seed Company, Post Falls, Idaho; Jeff Cox,
Kenwood, Calif.; Howard R. Crum and Vir-
ginia Crum, Lilypons Water Gardens, Buck-
eystown, Md.; Ashley Crumpton, Chapel
Hill, N.C.; Kenny Haddaway and Bob Hill,
Belmont Power Equipment, Newington,
Va.; Gerald W. Klancer, Woodbridge, Va.;
John Lewett and Mike Mayeux, J. L. Tree
Service, Fairfax, Va.; William T. Patton Sr.,
Turf Center Lawns, Inc., Silver Spring, Md.;
Louise S. Roberts, Chevy Chase, Md.; Alvin
Sacks, Bethesda, Md.; Pam Underhill,
Landscape, Arlington, Va.; Russell Whitt,
Silver Spring, Md.; David Yost, Virginia Co-
operative Extension, Fairfax, Va.

Christopher's Glen Echo Hardware, Glen
Echo, Md.; Hechinger, Gardening Department, Alexandria, Va.; Home Depot, Gardening Department, Alexandria, Va.; Merrifield Garden Center, Merrifield, Va.; Seven
Corners Rentals, Falls Church, Va.

**Library of Congress
Cataloging-in-Publication Data**
Landscaping / by the editors of Time-Life
  Books.
p.   cm. — (Home repair and improve-
  ment)
Includes index.
ISBN 0-7835-3879-0
1. Landscape gardening. I. Time-Life
  Books. II. Series.
SB473.L3693   1995
635.9—dc20   94-40921